The
Sharon Stone
Story

The
Sharon Stone
Story

Michael Munn

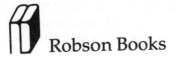

Robson Books

First published in Great Britain in 1997 by Robson Books Ltd, Bolsover House, 5–6 Clipstone Street, London W1P 8LE

British Library Cataloguing in Publication Data
A catalogue record for this title is available from the British Library

ISBN 1 86105 094 1

Photoset in North Wales by Derek Doyle & Associates, Mold, Flintshire. Printed in Great Britain by Hartnoll Ltd., Bodmin, Cornwall.

This book is
for Jane and Fred

Contents

Foreword

It may seem hard to believe that Sharon Stone has been a star for less than five years. But before 1992, before *Basic Instinct*, she had made scores of films since her debut in 1980. So she's actually been making movies for seventeen years, and has worked with a long list of leading actors and quite a few of the most respected directors in Hollywood.

As of 1996, she was the second biggest box-office female star in America, beaten only by Jodie Foster. The rest of Hollywood's leading ladies – even Demi Moore, Michelle Pfeiffer, Susan Sarandon, Sandra Bullock and Julia Roberts – all came below her in the top one hundred box-office stars, according to *Screen International*. In fact, in coming twentieth overall, she managed to beat some of the more dominant male stars who would most likely have been expected to reach positions higher up the charts.

In that same year she was awarded a Golden Globe as Best Actress and was nominated for an Oscar, both for *Casino*, and she received the best reviews of her career so far, also for *Casino*. So why did a lot of critics who said she surprised them by showing she could act in *Casino* go on to say later that she couldn't act when

reviewing *Last Dance*? I suggest that says more about the critics
than it does about Sharon Stone. Many of them continue to write
her off by insisting she is simply a sexy actress with no real acting
talent.

There are those in the film business who agree. Is that simply
because every other film she makes tends not to be liked by the
critics, or fails to become the biggest box-office attraction of the
year? Or does it say more about Hollywood than about her? I think
the story of her life and career sheds considerable light on
Hollywood, because making movies goes way beyond what the
public perceives it to be about or what the critics have to say.
Hollywood is a fascinating and dangerous place with its own rules
and moral guidelines, most of which are governed by two factors –
money and male supremacy – and while it has changed its rules
over the years, it remains locked into certain attitudes which have
affected Sharon's struggle to establish herself. Also, many of them
have also just disliked what she has had to say.

Never having been a particular fan of Sharon Stone myself, nor
of the films she made, I nevertheless decided to take a closer look
at her work and her life, and see what was going on. Just what kind
of *actress* is she to receive Hollywood's biggest accolades, yet be
written off so easily? What sort of *person* is she to be so mauled in
the media, and be called 'difficult' and even 'a bitch' by some who
have worked with her? And why does she seem to be forever having to prove herself again and again?

I had a head start at least – having interviewed her twice, and liking her enormously – though I remain aware from first-hand experience in this business that what you see is not always what is
behind the façade. Nevertheless, I must say she seemed genuine
and likeable. And very, very funny – which is certainly something
that has landed her in trouble, because what she says in person can
be made to look arrogant, contemptuous, even conceited when the
words appear in cold print, unless written by a sympathetic journalist.

The more I researched and wrote, and went back to the interviews I did with her and with others, the more I came to admire
her. As Robert Evans said, 'She's got balls like Mike Tyson.' And I

took a closer look at her films and found that while she is certainly not the best actress ever – and she never said she was – she is nevertheless far, far better than she has often been given credit for, as in *Casino*, worthy of the awards and accolades she has received.

She may yet surprise us all and become a great actress. Though as any actor knows, greatness only comes when you get the great parts provided by great writing and assisted by great direction. Film is too much of a collaborative art form for any individual to achieve the highest standards alone. So she will need those opportunities.

I am fortunate to have interviewed a number of people who worked with her over the years, including Richard Chamberlain, J. Lee-Thompson, Martin Scorsese, Michael Douglas, Robert Evans and Wes Craven, and I have drawn from those interviews in writing this book.

A special word of thanks goes to Kingsley Everett for his assistance in compiling and gathering additional research material.

1

The Fattest Thin Girl I Know

Joseph Stone was a good Pennsylvanian, raised to embrace Christian ethics and to respect womanhood. He was only four when his father died so it was left to his mother to raise him, but because she worked alternative night and day shifts in an institution, Joseph's upbringing was largely left in the very capable hands of his grandmother. He greatly loved his mother and grandmother, and grew to have immense respect for womanhood.

It was while still at high school, at the age of 15, that he met and fell in love for the first and only time with fellow classmate Dorothy. Within months they left school, and were married in 1950. They settled in the small Pennsylvanian town of Meadville – population around 15,000 – where Joseph went to work in the tool and die business, lifting and cutting steel blocks from three in the afternoon until eleven at night. Dorothy went back to school to finish her formal education, and then attended evening classes. When Joseph came home late each night, she taught him what she had learned that day before they went to bed.

Their first child, Michael, was born in 1951. It was another seven years before they had a second child, Sharon, born on 10th March 1958. While she would later spend much of her adolescent years trying to find a way to escape from the rural town, she would also acknowledge that it gave her a basic set of good home values which prepared her for the fast life, first as a model and later as a Hollywood star: 'Meadville was a very small town where everyone knew everybody else. I came from a solid, blue-collar family where I learned that good manners take you far. My upbringing left me with a basic way to live that saved my life when I was a young model living in Europe and New York – a lot of the girls I met then became drug addicts and died.'

Her mother discovered that her baby girl had a rather unusual talent which, at that time, Dorothy could never have imagined would prove to be a particular attribute for Sharon. Almost from the moment she could talk, she seemed to be consciously photogenic for, as her mother said, 'She was posing from the day she arrived. She came out posing. I have pictures of her where she's barely able to stand, and she has her hand up behind her head.'

While a child, Sharon found the country life a mixed blessing, especially for someone who was cursed – as she felt she was – with being unusually, *exceptionally* bright. She had what proved to be an IQ of 154, and was walking and talking at just ten months. 'I was never a kid,' she said. 'I was, like, forty at birth.' One jump ahead the day she started school, going straight into the second grade, she described herself as 'a real weird, academically driven kid, not at all interested in being social. I felt out of place. I was just so incredibly weird. I started school and drove everybody crazy because they realized I had popped out as an adult.' She plagued her teachers with questions that they didn't expect her to understand, let alone ask. When they tried to answer her in the simple way one would normally reply to a child, she demanded more meaningful responses. Her mother, she said, would just look horrified.

Dorothy was at a loss to know what to do with this exceptionally intelligent daughter who was so different from all the other children her age that her mother was actually scared. 'My Dad was among those who thought I was an alien,' said Sharon. 'My father was very rigid when we were young. If I was one minute late home, he was standing by the window. When I was a kid he was that "ugly guy". Since I had the ability to do things other kids didn't, he drove me towards perfection with a whip and a chair. That's very over-whelming. He's not like that now. He's the sweetest guy.'

Sharon's younger sister, Kelly, came along in 1961, and in 1966 her brother Patrick was born. Kelly said that when their father lost his temper, 'he would *really* lose his temper.' He didn't spare the rod, and when the kids knew they were going to get a spanking, they tried hiding books and comics down their pyjamas. But Joseph was not a tyrannical patriarch. He wanted his girls to stand on their own feet, and what he taught the boys he also taught the girls, including how to shoot. They became experienced in firing Magnums and high-powered hunting rifles; Kelly was a better shot than Sharon and earned the nickname 'Annie Oakley'.

Her older brother, Michael, recalled that Sharon was a 'tough lit-tle girl who knew how to shoot a rifle, fish and bait her own hook'. Said Joseph, 'Having been raised by women, I like to see women get a fair shot at life. They haven't for a long time.'

He had aspirations for Sharon, who didn't think she was special in any way; only that she was different. Bored with playing the nor-mal childhood games, she preferred to read during playtime at school. She was, she said, 'a nerdy ugly duckling. Success is mea-sured by how much you can be like everyone else at school. I always felt like an alien and was treated like one. To avoid going out, I'd hide in the back of the closet with a flashlight and read.' She came to think there was something wrong with her, as she was aware that she said and did things which made adults feel uncomfortable; at five, for example, she was correcting her mother's grammar. As a consequence, she was a very young misfit who just couldn't fit in.

Michael recalled, 'I've heard her refer to herself as a bit of a nerd because she was always into books. She was so gifted. You look at her pictures and you can see a certain brilliance about her.'

One of her great loves in life was to go to the movies. 'Ever since I was six, watching Fred Astaire and Ginger Rogers, I knew I was going to be an actress,' she said. In retrospect, the family realized it was no great surprise that eventually Sharon would become an actress. She began putting on plays in the family garage, using a sheet as a backcloth, and casting her sister and brothers in their roles; even as a child she was something of a small-scale 'mogul'.

She chose which plays they'd put on and directed them, while Dorothy helped the girls to make the costumes. They performed for the benefit of the neighbours, who came to see such classics as *Hansel and Gretel*.

Throughout early childhood, Sharon underwent various IQ tests. She was, she said, 'like a guinea pig or a hamster running round on a wheel. I put pegs in holes and matched colours with colours.' She took Rorschach tests and evaluative tests that suggested she was predisposed to sciences, engineering and maths. Her father told her, 'There's a great opportunity in engineering.'

She said, 'I'm sure a career as a chemist or an engineer would have been appropriate for me, though my personality is more fitting for a lawyer.' But at night, when Sharon and Kelly slept in twin beds in a room with sunflower wallpaper, they talked about their dreams: Kelly wanted to be a nurse, and Sharon wanted to be a movie star.

Whatever her father may have suggested would be ideal for her, Michael said, 'He always reinforced the thought with Sharon that she could do and have whatever she wanted in this world. He's never said to my sisters, "Honey, I think you should stay home and be someone's wife." '

All the testing just made her feel even 'more peculiar'. When she went to the nearest high school, at Seagertown, she moved speedily from one class to the next ahead of her peers. Because she was so singular in her abilities, and unable to make too many friends as she progressed through the grades faster than anybody else, she became a loner. Out of that situation she grew to become a rebel who began streaking through the school; it was the rebel more than the exhibitionist in her that drove her to do it. Also, that early streaking experience may have made it slightly easier for her when she had to do it to make a name for herself much later.

Although the Stones didn't live in poverty, they were far from affluent. Nevertheless, each Christmas the Stone children picked out their favourite toys and gave them to a poor family who lived nearby. 'We never resented it,' said Kelly. One year they gave the family the turkey which Joseph had received as a Christmas bonus.

When Joe fell ill, the family had to manage on meagre sickness payments. As Kelly recalled, 'It was a real struggle. We could barely afford luxuries at the best of times.' Even the necessities became scarce. Dorothy made many of their clothes; and while Joseph remained too ill to work, she made cornmeal mush. But they managed to survive until he was well enough to return to work on full pay.

Both Michael and Patrick were instilled with the 'solid blue-collar' philosophy of good manners. They opened doors for their sisters, and pulled out their chairs for them at the dinner table. But there was a wild streak in Michael, who was drinking at an early age – influenced, he said, by his 'hard-drinking' relatives. At that time, in the 1960s, it was a short jump to smoking marijuana. He said, 'Smoking a joint was small in comparison to being totally whacked out of your mind on alcohol.' At the age of 18 in 1969, he married his childhood sweetheart. Unhappily the bride's parents disapproved, which gave the marriage a rocky start from which it was unable to recover.

Living in a rural area, most of the Stones' neighbours had horses, and Sharon acquired a pony when she was 13 years old. It proved a skittish beast, and one day as she tried to ride it, it moved forward uncontrollably, sending her straight into a washing line which cut into her windpipe. Unable to escape from the line as the pony tried to keep going forward, she began gasping for breath; Dorothy arrived just in time to literally knock her from the pony. Sharon fell unconscious and was rushed to hospital with a suspected broken neck, but all she suffered was concussion and a dreadful cut on her neck that has left a lifelong scar.

Michael recalled, 'She nearly died. It was a horrible accident. She had terrible rope burn and almost choked to death. It left severe lacerations and she needed an operation.'

The girl who lived next door to the Stones, Dee Dee Snedeker, recalled the incident: 'We thought she'd broken her neck, but there were just cuts and bruises. Suddenly she saw the ambition to be a film star that she'd had from being a little girl going up in smoke, and it convinced her to stop taking wild chances that could stop her career before it started.'

For a long time Sharon was severely self-conscious about the injury. She didn't allow anyone to touch her neck, and applied thick make-up each morning to hide it before anyone saw her. It was a long while after the accident before she could bring herself to ride a horse.

Joseph laid down strict rules and forbade his daughters from dating until they were 16. At the age of 14, however, Sharon decided it was time to give her hormones a chance to get some exercise. There was a boy her own age who told her he'd teach her how to kiss, and they met secretly in the school auditorium during a free period. 'He sure taught me how to kiss, how to *feel* it, how to give someone room to kiss you back. I was very young and sexually immature then. I was always a great student, however!'

The boys were not, apparently, falling over themselves to date her. Sharon – tall, very thin, with dull fair hair and thick spectacles – was the plain one of the Stone sisters. She said, 'I had no sense of myself as a female.' Although Kelly was three years younger, she was the prettier one whom the boys wanted to go out with; Sharon they just ignored.

When she was 15, Sharon began paying attention to the way the female models in magazines dressed and posed, and she started reading articles on makeovers. 'I just looked at them and thought, "I can do that".' She dyed her fair hair black, then brown, then red; she finally settled on being blonde. Then she experimented with various styles of dress. She said, 'It was like a math problem. How do you get it to equal what you want?' As she grew in confidence, she bragged that she would replace Marilyn Monroe as the cinema's greatest blonde bombshell. Nobody believed her.

The 'nerdy ugly duckling' became an attractive 15-year-old. Sharon tried to do without her glasses, and eventually took to wearing contact lenses. She didn't use sugar or dairy fats, and never ate any of the hot dogs she sold to earn some cash. Said her one-time classmate and short-term teenage boyfriend Lou Severo:

She was the only teenage girl I ever met who was constantly on a diet. Not that she was ever an ounce overweight. You thought at first her obsession with watching what she ate was almost a problem. But it was obvious as soon as you talked to her what the reason behind it was. All she cared about was going to Hollywood and being a big movie star. At the time it sounded funny coming from a homely looking 15-year-old who wore too much make-up.

Her ambition to go to Hollywood was fed by a regular diet of movies. She recalled, 'There was only one movie theatre in my hometown, so I saw whatever was there a million times. I loved movies and painting and literature – everything artistic and aesthetic. It all inspired me. But my parents did not put me in a private school, so I didn't have the opportunity to achieve my full potential academically.'

Sharon and a few other bright students began attending nearby Edinboro State College each afternoon while still going to high school in the mornings. 'But, the college was not very stimulating,' she remembered.

She had very old-fashioned ideas about dating, and expected commitment from a boy who wanted to date her. Lou Severo saw her a few times, but he couldn't afford to buy her a ring out of his meagre earnings from his part-time job in a fast-food shop, so the romance was short-lived. Nevertheless, they stayed good friends for many years.

Wanting to make sure that his girls could stand on their own two feet in all things, Joseph wouldn't allow them to get a driver's license until they could change a wheel by themselves, so he taught them how to fix cars and bought Sharon a Ford Escort. But she had barely learned to drive when, in 1974, she crashed it. An eyewitness, Jimmy Tonko, said, 'It was a bitter winter day in 1974 and her old Ford hit an ice patch a few blocks away from her house. She was thrown from the car and narrowly missed hitting a tree with her head, which would definitely have killed her.'

Sharon was rushed to hospital where Dee Dee came to see her: 'She was miserable with her face all puffed up, black and blue. But she was a survivor and tough. You would never accuse Sharon of being a delicate girl. She kept her sense of humour and survived the ordeal.'

Now an attractive teenager, Sharon should have been competing with her pretty younger sister for the boys' attention, but as Kelly recalled it, 'It was me the boys came to see. Sharon was always too busy with her head in a book.'

Sharon had her first real love affair with Craig Grindell, Jnr, who came from a rich family that owned several factories in the Meadville area. Craig, a handsome young man who drove a $35,000 Corvette sports car, did what he liked and listened to no one. Sharon, desperate to find a way to escape the dull life of a small rural town, was excited by the young rebel.

Then Craig was killed in a horrific car crash. Lou Severo was there on the night, and recalled, 'I was out with a bunch of guys drinking and drag racing on a stretch of country road. Craig was very drunk and wanted to prove his Corvette was the fastest car in town.' Craig drove his car at around 100 miles an hour, straight into a concrete barrier. 'The car disintegrated,' remembered Severo. 'Craig's passenger was thrown more than 200 feet but Craig was burned beyond recognition in a fireball.'

Dee Dee said, 'Sharon was inconsolable. She might have married him. At the funeral she was so grief-stricken she had to be supported or she'd have fallen to the ground.' But, as Dee Dee had observed, Sharon was tough and a survivor – her young life was certainly proving tough to survive.

Her boast that she would supersede Monroe was no mere dream without substance. Sharon was very active in the school's theatre productions. 'She was always confident on stage and there was a spark, but I never thought – there was no indication – that she was going to be the hottest movie star in the world,' said Richard Baker, who was the assistant principal at Seagertown High School.

She graduated to college full-time in 1975, gaining a scholarship based on her writing abilities. The Dean was very flexible towards her because of her academic gifts. As she remembered:

He let me take course overloads, and I didn't have to be in all my classes all the time, so long as I maintained a certain grade point average. The classes were very helpful to me, but it soon became clear that I could take a course overload and drugs and *still* be bored. I needed to be in a different environment in order to be inspired to go on with academics. I took a course in history of modern architecture, in which I learned about Christo. I ended up minoring in modern architecture because it was so inspiring to me to think of artists as architects and architects as artists. It was a revelation that an artist wasn't defined by his medium.

She also said that 'of all the arts I thought I had the least talent as an actor – so I picked it. It was the furthest to reach.' Meanwhile, she continued to work on her appearance to give herself a more glamorous image. Lou Severo said that he saw her a few years after she started college 'and was amazed. She'd completely remade herself as a beauty. A lot of the guys who had dated her casually were sorry they hadn't taken her more seriously.'

She taught herself how to stand, how to move; she even worked on her smile. One of her girlfriends, Linda Bidwell Simcheck, recalled, 'She was pretty – and she knew it. I am not saying she was conceited – but she was a little.' Her Dean said, 'She was clearly the prettiest girl as well as the brightest. Girls were terribly jealous of her.'

Kelly now found herself having to compete with Sharon for attention, and flirted with every college boy who took an interest in her older sister. Kelly admitted, 'When it came to boys, Sharon was much choosier than me.' Her father Joseph was also choosy; he stood in the kitchen to view boyfriends through the window when they came courting Sharon. He disliked boys with long hair, and on one occasion when he saw a long-haired youth come calling, he said, 'What do you want, Long Hair? I hope you're not considering taking Sharon out looking like *that*!'

Despite the fact that Sharon had become a beauty and enjoyed being courted, she was very straitlaced about dating and far from the sexually driven woman that people would later perceive her to be because of the film roles she played. Kelly was a virgin until she was 18, but she recalled that Sharon was much older. 'She simply wasn't interested.'

Sharon always felt that a man's sexiest attribute was his lips. 'It is often the lips that do it for me,' she said. 'Big, full lips.'

When she was 17 she began going out with 18-year-old local football star Ray Butterfield. Sharon was thrilled that he had a motorbike, but unlike Craig, Ray was not reckless. His mother, Joyce, recalled, 'A mother always wants her son to go out with a nice girl and I approved of Sharon. They were so very much in love. They often used to go out in a crowd to the movies or a ball game. But mainly they used to go out on his bike.'

Other times they'd be at his house listening to music, and if they were apart they'd be on the phone to each other. There was a time when Sharon had felt too 'nerdy' to go to the school prom, but in 1975 she went with Ray. Two months later he ran his motorbike off the road and died instantly.

Kelly recalled, 'Sharon was crying so hard the day he died. It was a tragedy for the whole town.' Ray's mother said:

> They were very much in love. I'm surprised Sharon wasn't on the bike the night he died. They were usually on it together. We never did find out why he ran off the road. Sharon was in total shock for weeks after the accident. She couldn't stop crying at the funeral. I held her in my arms and she sobbed 'I loved him so much.' If Ray had lived, I'm certain their relationship would have developed into something permanent.

The normal happy, family-oriented life of the Stones was shaken in 1975 when Michael's marriage broke apart. He had a young son, Brian, born that year. But the disapproval of his wife's parents and his foray into drugs took their toll. He was divorced, and his life became even wilder as he drank heavily and began taking cocaine.

Sharon began dating Richard Baker Jnr, son of the high school assistant principal. Richard shared her love of films and theatre, but he had a rather moody disposition and seemed not to share her sense of humour. She often told him and his parents that she was going to be the new Monroe. Richard's mother, Pauline, said, 'Sharon always had the big "A" – for ambition. She saw her way out of Meadville.'

In 1975 Sharon entered the Miss Crawford County beauty pageant. She later insisted that someone else had put her name forward, but some of her old friends seemed to think that she did this herself. She chose to recite the Gettysburg Address and asked a neighbour, Walter Holland, an eye surgeon, to coach her. On the day, Walter's wife, Hap, took Sharon to one side and began to impress upon her the horrors of the American Civil War to get her to put some real feeling into the recital. 'She seemed to be hanging on every word,' Hap Holland recalled. 'She was animated and nodding, and appeared to be getting the message.'

Then they went over to where Walter was waiting, and Hap smiled as a signal that her chore had been accomplished. After Hap had run over a few more things about the seriousness and depth of tragedy of the war, Sharon said very solemnly, 'Mrs Holland, may I ask you something?'

'Certainly, dear. What is it?'

'Should I wear sparkly stuff in my hair?'

Hap Holland paused thoughtfully for a moment before answering, wondering if she had been getting through, and said, 'Yes, dear, that would be a good idea.' So Sharon Stone wore 'sparkly stuff', gave her address and became Miss Crawford County of 1975. Part of her prize was an invitation to compete for Miss Pennsylvania in Philadelphia. Sharon had never been outside her community: 'I'd never done anything. It wasn't until I was a senior in high school that I went on an escalator for the first time. When I went to Philadelphia I had never been in an elevator before.'

She didn't become Miss Pennsylvania – in fact she didn't even come third or second – but one of the judges was sufficiently impressed to suggest to Dorothy that Sharon ought to try modelling. The prospect of modelling wasn't the thing that particularly excited Sharon – it was the prospect of escaping from her drab life. And Marilyn Monroe had been a model before becoming a movie star . . . .

Sharon applied to the Eileen Ford Model Agency, and finally got a call, asking her to come for an interview in New York just before

Christmas 1976. Before she left Meadville, her mother told her, 'If they don't like you, you can come back here and hit the books.'

But Sharon replied, 'If they don't like me, I'll just try someplace else.'

She went up to the city and was overawed by it. At her interview with the Eileen Ford Model Agency, they accepted her and put her on their books. She returned home, but only to announce that she was embarking on a modelling career. Kelly recalled, 'We were not close when we were young. When she left home to model in New York, I looked up to her, but I was working as a nurse and we had little in common.'

Aged 18, Sharon said goodbye to her family and to Richard Baker, Jnr, and went back to New York where she took up residence in an apartment owned by the agency: in all respects it was a dormitory where they could keep her under strict supervision. Under constant pressure to become thinner, she was put on a diet of crackers and water, even soda drinks were banned. She said, 'To them I was a big farm girl. I was the fattest thin girl I knew.'

Once her career was under way, treading the catwalks of New York, she was earning enough to move out of the dorm and into an apartment down town. Next came the move to Europe and a life of globe-trotting, earning up to $500 a day. But it became a dark period in her life.

2

A New Bombshell Lands in Hollywood

'I still find it hard to believe I have modelled everywhere, from Manhattan to Milan, Paris to Japan, South Africa to Hollywood,' said Sharon. Throughout the whole of her modelling career, she never gave up the dream of being a film star.

She had a thrifty attitude towards money and, from the time she began modelling, she invested in savings and pension schemes. She always believed that it was the good home values she'd been instilled with that kept her from going off the rails like some of the other models in Europe. Some became drug addicts, and many of those who did so died.

In 1978 she was in Rome. At that time the city was under a reign of terror from the Marxist group the Red Brigade, which tried to overthrow the government by kidnapping, kneecapping and killing people. 'It was a really scary time,' she said. 'There was this kind of intensity everywhere in such a small country that everybody feels politically involved or active.' She would later make a film about the Red Brigade, *Year of the Gun*.

She continued to work throughout Europe and was forever plagued by European playboys. In Milan she found the Italians were among the worst, where she wasn't so much wooed but

13

'tortured' as she put it. Eventually she wondered to herself, 'Why am I doing this?' There was no good answer except that she wanted to be an actress more than a model. So she packed her bags and returned to New York, where she studied method acting with Marilyn Freid and Jack Waltzer while continuing to earn good money as a model.

Sharon very nearly succumbed to the intense pressures of modelling when she went to a so-called 'doctor' in Manhattan who said he could take away her bulges. He injected her every day with animal hormones which were supposed to change her metabolism. The daily shots left her feeling dizzy and weak, and she finally became so ill that she was convinced she was dying; she shook violently, her head throbbed unbearably, and she couldn't walk. A friend managed to get her to a genuine doctor, who was unable to diagnose what was wrong because Sharon wouldn't tell him about the injections. He decided to check her straight into a hospital, but she protested and got her friend to take her home, where she remained very sick until finally the effects of the shots wore off.

It was only a little later that she discovered the injections she had been given all that time were compiled from sheep embryos and urine from pregnant women. She long realized that she was lucky to survive what she considered to be the darkest period of her life. 'I didn't know the depths of darkness to which I would fall. Some of the girls I was with are dead now. The late seventies and early eighties were very decadent times. People were free-basing cocaine, partying all night long and having wild sex. I wasn't into that. I would go to the clubs all night and drink mineral water. It was like working out for me.'

She was acutely aware of the pitfalls of drugs, for her brother Michael was arrested in 1979 for possessing cocaine and sent to New York's Attica Prison for two years. He later admitted, 'I was a marijuana smuggler in the seventies. I deserved to go to jail. I thought I could beat the system.' He credited Sharon with helping him through it all, as she stuck by him and encouraged him to clean up his act.

Sister Kelly had achieved her lifelong ambition to be a nurse, and their father finally went into business for himself as an engineer. 'I tried to make things a little more comfortable for my kids,' he said. 'I worked in a machine shop for thirty years before I started my own business. Took a long time.'

Over three years, Sharon rose to become one of the agency's top ten models, and during that time she had to fend off the many lechers that infested the business. When she later starred as the ice-pick-wielding Catherine Tramell in *Basic Instinct*, she said, 'During my time as a model, I would have loved to have killed a lot of art directors and clients I worked with over the years. To have ice-picked them as they came into the changing room every time we were changing . . .!'

Those three years were a life-learning experience that prepared her for what awaited in Hollywood. As well as preparing to be an actress with lessons in such things as movement and posture, she also learned how to deal with predatory men.

Her mother, who came to visit her in New York from time to time, was horrified that her little girl had not only grown up much but had become a whole new person. Said Dorothy, 'When I'd go out in the street with her in New York, she'd put her fingers in her mouth and whistle for a cab. I'd look at her and think, "Who is this girl?" I was frightened to death, but it was like she had been there all her life.'

After three years Sharon became desperate to give up modelling altogether. 'Being in that world always seemed like such a scam to me. I was always uncomfortable. But at the same time I was able to do it and make great money, so that I didn't have to be a starving artist while I studied acting and lost my Pennsylvanian accent. I made the jump to acting because modelling is so demeaning to the women who do it.'

Her beginning as an actress was not auspicious. She appeared in scores of TV commercials, including ads for Diet Coke and Clairol. Then she heard that Woody Allen was about to make *Stardust Memories*, and was looking for an unknown actress to play a very small role. When Sharon turned up at a high school where he was conducting the auditions in the cafeteria, she found herself just one of hundreds; Allen sat with his casting director as the girls were virtually paraded. He later explained what kind of girl he was looking for: 'I needed someone who would look startling, but not comic-book. I wanted a real fantasy woman.'

As agents had sent so many girls along, Allen and his casting director had to whittle the numbers down. Meanwhile, Sharon sat reading a children's book she'd picked up, which explained infinity. Virtually all of the girls were dismissed, and she recalled, 'I sat there for a while, watching hundreds of others hand in their pictures. Woody never spoke to me. After a while I thought, "Fellini should be shooting this. I'm gonna go now".' And so she walked over to Woody Allen with all the poise and grace of an experienced model, gave him her picture, and walked away. Shortly after, the casting director came up to her and said, 'Mr Allen wants you to stay.'

Woody went over to her and asked about the book she was reading, and they spent the next half-hour discussing the subject of infinity. Then he left, and the casting director came over to tell Sharon, 'Hey, Woody really liked you. Would you like to have a part in the movie?' Sharon recalled, 'I'm like, "All *right*! When do I start?"'

All the time Sharon and Woody had been discussing infinity, he had been making up his mind whether she was what he was looking for. He explained, 'I looked at her and thought I would *really* like her to kiss me!' That's all he needed to know.

Sharon was sent to wardrobe and they put her in what she described as 'a blonde bombshell dress'. She said, 'Wait, let me explain something. I'm not a bombshell.' But as she later recalled it, 'They didn't see it my way.'

She said, 'You have to understand that I was twenty-two and looked sixteen and had this voice and this attitude. There was nowhere for me. The best slot that people felt they could put me in was the bimbo shot. It's because I looked like Barbie.'

At the time of *Stardust Memories*, Allen was still developing his reputation as a highly respected film-maker, having begun as a club comedian and comedy screenwriter in the 1960s. During the 1970s he had written, directed and starred in some of his most enduring classics, particularly *Play It Again Sam*, and his semi-autobiographical New York pictures *Annie Hall* and *Manhattan*. *Stardust Memories* was to be more autobiographical than ever. He played Sandy Bates, a comedy actor and film director attending a weekend retrospective of his films, hosted by real-life American film critic Judith Crist. He finds himself the target of various people in the audience who demand to know why he doesn't make funny films like he used to. Like the real Woody Allen, Bates has turned to making more meaningful, retrospective and somewhat autobiographical films.

In a series of flashbacks, Bates's bumpy relationships are revealed, one with Isobel, played by Marie-Christine Barrault, a married Frenchwoman with two children who is on the verge of divorce, and another with beautiful but highly strung actress Dorrie, played by Charlotte Rampling.

The last part of the picture is a 'film within a film' as the weekend audience watches his latest, most difficult and soul-searching film to date, in which he plays a character who has a close encounter with aliens. He asks them what he should do for the benefit of mankind, and they tell him to make funnier films. *Stardust Memories* was even less of a comedy than his earlier pictures, but was an incisive and perceptive attack on critics and film executives who were asking him the same question Bates was being asked; why wasn't he making funny films like *Take the Money and Run*, *Bananas* and *Everything You Always Wanted to Know About Sex*?

When he came to make *Stardust Memories* there was the thought that he might have peaked, or gone too far, and if that was so and the film turned out to be a disaster, then as far as Sharon's own career was concerned, it could have been over before it began. Not that she was thinking of this at the time – a part in a film was a part in a film – and she wasn't about to question the wisdom of doing it. It was a now-or-never opportunity. And so she made her film debut in Woody Allen's black and white *Stardust Memories* in 1980.

She was billed as 'pretty girl on the train', and appeared in a single scene in which Allen, as Bates, is taking a train journey when he sees his fantasy woman through the window. She was dressed in a silk 1930s sheath dress – the 'blonde bombshell dress' – and marabou feathers, with her hair twined in a Betty Grable topknot. He sees her being handed a trophy, and finds he wants her so much. He dreams that she kisses him, but the window frame is between them.

When she came to shoot the scene, Allen told her that he wanted her to kiss the window, 'but do it like you were really kissing me'. She later said, 'I kissed the window like I really meant it!'

The film certainly gave the critics and Allen's regular audience something to think about. 'Though there are laughs along the way,' said *Variety*, 'this is a truly mean-spirited picture. Once a sympathetic nebbish, Allen sees himself as a put-upon, embittered genius, disdainful of everything around him.' Gilbert Adair in the *Monthly Film Bulletin* thought the film's 'posturing pyrotechnics seem more the symptom of a crisis than its controlled expression'.

Film Review took a more lenient view, saying that Allen had 'come up with a film that will even give his most ardent fans cause to furrow their brows', and commented, 'though it has its fair share of laughs, it is an iconoclastic, thought-provoking stab at autobiography . . . . It isn't an easy film to follow, and bound to cause a polemic on a grand scale, but it is a brave attempt at pushing cinematic narrative one step nearer to art.'

Despite a less than enthusiastic critical response, the film made them sit up and take notice, which is perhaps all Allen wanted them to do. Not that Sharon, in her brief appearance, was going to be noticed by the critics, but she did get noticed by an agent to whom she was a typical 'pretty young thing' with blonde hair who should be able to get work in typical 'pretty young thing' roles. That, though, was not part of her long-term, and if possible short-term, plan. But as they say, the best-laid plans . . .!

Allen said some years later, after Sharon had achieved stardom, 'You take a chance on a moment and a person and hope it works. This one did quite wonderfully. All these years later, Sharon's a whole new business but I'd like to work with her again. Maybe we could have a real kiss this time.'

After that film, she decided to make the move to Hollywood. 'I took everything I owned and got an apartment on the coast at Marina Del Ray, which I'd agreed to take by looking at Polaroids. But it was tacky and horrible. I realized then that I was going to have to be successful to pay for something better.'

Sharon continued her acting studies, going to the Tracy Roberts Acting Workshop and the Harvey Lembeck Improvisational Comedy Workshop. She also took private lessons from actor Allan Rich. Then she had lessons under Roy London, and said, 'I don't think I really learned anything until I began studying with Roy London in Los Angeles. He has an intellectual approach to acting. He doesn't tell you to lie down on the floor and pretend to be a piece of bacon frying.'

When London asked her what she wanted to achieve, she told him, 'I want to be good enough to work with Robert De Niro.'

In 1993 she reflected, 'When I was young, all I wanted to be was a movie star. At a certain point I started to grow up and really care about what I did. When I had studied acting with Roy London for years, I lost all the pretence about movie stars.'

It was more the fact that she had 'the bimbo and Barbie' look than her developing acting abilities that began getting her small film roles. Her second film was *Deadly Blessing*, directed by Wes Craven who specialized in cheap, gory horror flicks. He had started his directing career inauspiciously with a TV movie *Stranger In Our House* (also known as *Summer of Fear*) in 1978, which starred Linda Blair, but had gained a cult following with *The Hills Have Eyes* in 1979, establishing his penchant for story twists, excessive gore and plenty of pretty girls in peril from evil. When Sharon got the part in *Deadly Blessing* it wasn't for her acting; neither was it a well-planned career move. She was offered the part and could not afford to turn it down. It was to be just one in a long line of films that she described as 'crap'.

'I worked really hard because I was pulling such a heavy load when the films weren't good, and you knew they weren't going to be any good,' she said later.

In *Deadly Blessing*, old-timer Ernest Borgnine played the head of a repressed religious sect amongst whose congregation is a man who cannot resist the arrival of a visiting sexy widow and her equally sexy friends. Among the good-time girls is a drug-addicted model who becomes one of the murderous stalker's victims; that was Sharon's part. The cast included Jeff East (who played the young Clark Kent in *Superman The Movie*), Maren Jensen, Susan

Buckner and Lois Nettleton. Sharon called the film *'Charlie's Angels Get a Scare'*, saying her role as a beautiful blonde model was 'not unlike my natural self at the time'. It might have helped if *Deadly Blessing* had turned out to be a cult classic like *The Hills Have Eyes*, but it was a forgettable film, unlike the one Wes Craven made three years later – *Nightmare on Elm Street*. On the other hand, had it done so, Sharon might well have become the 1980s 'Queen of Scream'. In retrospect, the failure of the film may not have been an altogether unmixed blessing.

Wes Craven was more impressed with her than she was with his film, and he said:

> She wasn't looking for an easy way to succeed. She was willing to work, to take classes, and do all she could as long as she could be a star. Would-be actors and actresses come out to Hollywood all the time and think it is easy. But it's not. You can be the most beautiful girl in the world, but if you can't put presence or charisma or whatever that star 'it' is over on screen, it doesn't matter how gorgeous you are. Sharon had 'it'. There was never any question.

He also saw how she 'set goals months and years ahead and everything she does is pointed in that direction'.

In those early days in Hollywood, Sharon came up against the inevitable casting couch. Her first experience was with a studio executive who was so furious when she refused to have sex with him that he actually yelled, 'You'll never work in this town again!' She recalled, 'It was the funniest thing I'd ever *heard*.'

There was another experience when a producer unzipped his fly and showed her what he was going to give to her. She recalled, 'I thought that was the funniest thing I'd ever *seen*. I mean, hey, if you're going to act out a movie, couldn't you at least act out a better one?'

Steven Bochco was the name behind some of the best American drama series of the past decade, including *Hill Street Blues*, *LA Law* and *NYPD Blue*. One of his earlier shows was a baseball drama, *Bay City Blues*, for NBC. Sharon landed a central role as a baseball player's wife and suddenly found herself with a contract for twenty-one episodes and financial security. The fear of being stuck in a TV part for years was the least of her worries. She went to work on it and several episodes were filmed; but it was short-lived, failing to find a big enough audience and being cancelled by NBC before it really had a chance to take off. At least Sharon was paid well, even for the episodes that didn't get made.

Her disappointment dispelled with time. The cancellation of the show saved her from becoming identifiable strictly as a TV star, as has happened to so many actors. It is doubtful that she would have ever been allowed to go on to become the sexy star of *Basic Instinct* had *Bay City Blues* been a success. It was simply the case – and still is – that TV stars, with very rare exceptions, do not become major international movie stars.

Sharon continued to work hard at her drama classes and went up for every audition she was offered. Even though many beautiful blondes were, and are, able to make a living in films before gravity and age bring early retirement, she quickly learned to appreciate the value of her acting classes. 'I'm one of the few blondes in the business who has trained hard dramatically and comedically. You have to work hard, because when you walk into an auditorium you had better have something to give the casting director. Auditions are nerve-racking enough. One of my strong points was that I'm so chameleon like in my looks that it's hard for a producer to pinpoint my age. I'm also relatively articulate.'

She appeared very fleetingly in *Bolero* – not the infamous Bo Derek-John Derek production of 1984 but the French film directed by Claude Lelouch in 1981. Lelouch had directed a number of very fashionable and visually stylish films during the 1960s, notably *Un Homme et Une Femme* (*A Man and a Woman*) and *Vivre Pour Vivre* (*Live for Life*). He continued to make films into the 1980s, including *A Man and A Woman: 20 Years Later*.

He chose an international cast for *Bolero*, namely James Caan, Geraldine Chaplin, Jean-Claude Brialy, Nicole Garcia, Daniel Olbrychski and Robert Hossein. Most of the actors played more than one character in what was a tedious and confusing saga of a whole host of characters and their love of music. The story covered a time span of fifty years and ran for almost three hours, although in France, where it was called *Les Uns et les Autres*, it ran in a six-hour version. It was just a quick job for Sharon, who was missed if anyone blinked. Had the film become a classic, at least she might have been able to boast that she had been in it, but by the time it was made Claude Lelouch was well past his best, and even his 1986 sequel to *A Man and a Woman* failed to re-establish him.

In 1984 she had her best role so far in *Irreconcilable Differences*, written by husband-and-wife team Charles Shyer and Nancy Meyers. This was a sweet-and-sour romantic comedy about Albert Brosky, a professor of film who goes from teaching about film to producing one which, to everyone's surprise, becomes a fluke hit. Getting caught up in the trappings of tinsel town, he takes to Hollywood and abandons his wife and nine-year-old daughter, while he sets about trying to make waitress Blake Chandler into a film star by casting her as Scarlett O'Hara in a musical remake of *Gone With the Wind*. The result, *Atlanta*, proves to be a disaster. Meanwhile, the daughter attempts to divorce herself from her parents.

The film was a directorial debut for Charles Shyer, who wrote *Private Benjamin* with wife Nancy Meyers; together they scripted this one too. Ryan O'Neal starred as Bordsky, with Shelley Long as his wife. Drew Barrymore played the daughter, and in the role of waitress Blake Chandler was Sharon Stone. The film is structured around the court case and – using testimony and, of course, flash-backs – we get to examine O'Neal and Long's relationship from their first meeting, through marriage and to the eventual break-down of their relationship.

O'Neal felt the film was a brave attempt at a comedy about Hollywood because 'everybody in Hollywood was scared to make a movie about a Hollywood director who leaves his wife and kid for a starlet. Everybody was going to think it was about them.'

The screenplay was, apparently, inspired by a real-life producer. When Ryan O'Neal told the story of the film to Gregory Peck, Peck responded with, 'I know any number of directors who have done that.' Certainly the sharp and funny script was an incisive satire on the movie business, and the performances of O'Neal and Long were particularly appealing.

It was also a fine early role for Sharon, who displayed much promise in a part that might have been a typical bimbo but was played with satire. Anyone who might have thought Sharon was just playing herself was mistaken. She prepared by watching old films such as *His Girl Friday* with Cary Grant and Rosalind Russell, and *To Have and Have Not* with Humphrey Bogart and Lauren Bacall. Charles Shyer said, 'I wanted Sharon to see Bacall's debut. I thought she was someone who was going to reach the same heights in the movies. She had a gift for timing and comic delivery. She had all the right qualities. And the determination to make a success of her role and the movie. She wanted all of us to be winners.'

Sharon described her character as 'an actress who doesn't realize that every time she breaks into song in a musical she's really *stupid*'. She recalled that the studio screened two Cybill Shepherd films for her. This was her most enjoyable experience as an actress so far. 'The film was so much fun. I loved doing it.'

Irreconcilable Differences was relatively inexpensive by Hollywood standards, costing just under $6 million. O'Neal received no salary but was on a percentage deal. He said of Sharon, 'She was exceptional in a tough role, and there was no doubt that one day she was going to be a remarkable star.'

Unfortunately the film was not well received. *Variety* noted that it 'begins strongly as a human comedy about a nine-year-old who decides to take legal action to divorce her parents. Unfortunately, this premise is soon jettisoned for a rather familiar tale of a marriage turned sour. Set in the world of Hollywood writers and filmmakers, the story is also more fun for the cognoscenti than the average filmgoer.' It also disliked the story being structured around the court case, 'an uninspired and improbable device to tell the yarn . . . . Ryan O'Neal and Shelley Long spark off a nice romantic chemistry but really need a better vehicle to show off their craft.'

However, Scot Haller wrote in *People*, 'When Stone belts a brassy Streisand-like number amid the corpses after the burning of Atlanta, the comedy shows a fresh sensibility.'

And Virgin's *Film Year Book 1986* liked it. 'What could have been another tedious tug-of-love saga is jiffed up by a witty script and amiable performances into a wry look at Hollywood lifestyles and the excesses of fame, complete with film industry in-jokes and intriguing peeks at the screenwriting process.'

It wasn't so much the failure of the film that ultimately disappointed Sharon, but what was generally going on in her career. She said, 'Even though I got a tremendous amount of attention, and great reviews from the part, my career was really improperly managed at the time. The mistakes that were made cost me many years of having to make shitty movies.'

She also found it virtually impossible to make her opinions known, observing, 'You just cannot be blonde with a good body and pretty looks *and* have any opinions in Hollywood. They don't like it if you turn out to have any amount of intelligence. To the boys who run things, you're just a dumb blonde, so you'd better know your place.'

Going on the adage, 'If you can't beat them join them,' she used the image people perceived her to be to her advantage. She said, 'Being blonde is a great excuse when you are having a bad day. "I'm blonde, I can't help it – I'm just feeling very *blonde* today." ' With her usual humour, she added, 'I do try to lie on my back in black lingerie as often as possible!'

In 1984 Sharon was in the TV movie *The Vegas Strip Wars*. She took the part because it was work, it was experience, and nothing much better was being offered at the time.

One-time movie idol Rock Hudson was the star. Since the 1970s, when he was back at his old studio, Universal, making the TV series *McMillan and Wife*, he had been virtually relegated to television. *The Vegas Strip Wars* was to be his last TV feature movie.

He played a maverick casino owner who wages war on the partners who have double-crossed him. James Earl Jones provided an outrageous performance in an equally outrageous fright wig as a fight promoter who was not unlike real promoter Don King. Sharon had a good-sized role, providing the main female interest, as a cigarette girl who seduces Hudson, manipulating him for her own ends through her sexual power. The film wasn't up to much, but she had a chance to show that she could play a part other than a mere bimbo while displaying something of the sexual chemistry that would eventually make her into a star.

Although the film itself would never be a life-changing movie for anyone who watched it, it did change Sharon's life. The producer was Michael Greenburg, who, like all TV producers, wanted to become a feature film producer. He was a handsome man, rather gentle for someone in his profession but very craftsmanlike in his work. She said she loved him from the minute she set eyes on him. And the feeling was mutual. They began spending a lot of time together on and off the set; it was her first real love affair since leaving Meadville, and she seemed to accept that at the age of 25 she was soon going to become a married woman, mainly becuse that's what proper young ladies did when they fell in love.

She called her parents and told them, 'I've met the man of my dreams,' suggesting her father should buy a new suit and her mother 'something very special' in anticipation of a wedding. She was, they later said, as excited 'as a little girl'.

The film had another profound effect on Sharon. Everyone in the business knew by then that Rock Hudson was a homosexual, but for years he had been compelled to hide his sexuality from the public. He had been the heart-throb of millions of women during the 1950s, when he was at the height of his popularity; had word got out that he was gay, his career would have been over. There was intolerance towards homosexuals, not so much from the industry – there have always been many gays in the film and theatre business – but from the media and the public. A lot of the great directors were gay, as were some stars, both male and female. But because of the way the studio star system worked, these people were both protected and somewhat imprisoned. Sham weddings were often arranged by the studios, as in the case of Rock Hudson. It was not frowned upon by Hollywood to *be* gay – just to be *known* to be gay.

All that changed with AIDS, and Rock Hudson became its first known celebrity victim. His illness helped to spread the cause being advanced by homophobic individuals and organizations who dubbed AIDS 'The Gay Plague'. It was, claimed some religious groups, God's retribution for their terrible sin. The fact was, a lot worse had long gone on in Hollywood, from outright criminal activity such as drug-running, blackmail and even murder, not to mention being in league with the Mafia during the 1930s and 1940s. Perhaps even the greed and often plain cruelty of Hollywood were sins with which those groups should have been more concerned.

Because of the much-vaunted self-righteous propaganda over the so-called 'Gay Plague', it became necessary again for Rock Hudson to keep a secret, even from Hollywood. By the time he came to make *The Vegas Strip Wars* he knew he was going to die. But he didn't burden others with the knowledge although, when it was revealed, there were those he had worked with who became most alarmed that he hadn't told them – not always out of concern for him but for themselves, mainly through what was then a significant and understandable ignorance about the disease.

Hudson was a warm personality, much loved by many of the actresses he had worked with such as Elizabeth Taylor and Carroll Baker, and he was not, as has been said, detested by all the he-man actors of Hollywood. It was not surprising, therefore, that Sharon became very fond of him, and he of her. She knew he was gay, but she probably didn't know he had AIDS. They spent time away from the set telling each other their troubles, and he talked about the secret life he had had to live in the closet. He told her that his housekeeper said to him, 'Talk about coming out of the closet – you came out of the house!' It remained her favourite Rock Hudson story.

They had such a warm and immediate friendship that they made a pact that when she had her first child, he would be its godfather. She said later, after his death in 1985, 'Rock was an extraordinary brave and generous man. We became very good friends. It was a special time for me.'

Sharon and Michael were married on 18th August 1984, in Erie, Pennsylvania. It was just a small ceremony. They returned to Beverly Hills to live in a rented apartment where crystals and collected art pieces were evidence of their joint affluence. 'It was like one of those apartments they show you to see what yours *could* be like,' said Greenburg's production associate Tina Livingstone. The joint incomes of Mr and Mrs Greenburg were enough to provide a BMW 325E for her and an Alfa Romeo for him. They had, she said, 'A sort of squeaky-clean little relationship. I wanted us to be the perfect couple.'

As in all good Hollywood love stories, there were various anonymous 'friends' who said that Sharon and Michael made 'the perfect couple' and that they were 'devoted to each other'. The fact was, as Sharon would later admit, 'I pretty much knew on my honeymoon that I was screwed.' She also later commented with typical Stone wit, 'He had no lips – he was the antithesis of my lips fixation!'

Their one true shared interest was movies; they went to see every film on the day it opened. But the next twelve months were to prove that living together and working together was not always indicative of happiness – not even if those twelve months were spent in a place like Africa.

3

In and Out of Africa

The Cannon group wanted to make two big adventure films to rival Steven Spielberg's Indiana Jones movies in 1985. The plan was to remake *King Solomon's Mines* and its sequel *Allan Quartermain and the Lost City of Gold*, and do it the way Alexander and Ilya Salkind had made their successful twin movies – *The Three Musketeers* and *The Four Musketeers*, and their first two *Superman* films – literally, back to back.

Cannon was a relatively new company, operating from London with Elstree Studios as its home base. It was run by Menahem Golan and Yorum Globus, two fairly formidable film names during the 1980s. Golan, in particular, was a highly respected director born and bred in the former Palestine. He had worked for a while as an assistant to Roger Corman, where he learned the art of making profitable cheapies. In the early 1960s he returned to Israel to produce and direct his own films very successfully, forming his own production company, Noah. Then he went into partnership with Yorum Globus, an Israeli film producer, and they set out to conquer the American market in 1974 by making the much underrated *Lepke*, a gangster picture starring Tony Curtis as the Jewish mobster who was the only one of 'Lucky' Luciano's Mafia-backed gang to go to the electric chair.

The Golan/Globus partnership made several other interesting if not hugely successful films, including the Israeli version of the raid on Entebbe airport, *Operation Thunderbolt*. Moving their base to London, they set up Cannon Films with the intention of producing highly commercial star-studded action films. But somehow they just didn't have the flair nor the fortune to harvest great profits, and many of their films were second- and third-rate competitors in the international market. Which was a great shame because they were, in effect, trying to give the British film industry a much-needed shot in the arm, but only managed to wither along with the rest of the British production companies. In 1990 Cannon was bought by Giancarlo Parretii, described by *Variety* as 'the Italian-born mystery man', who changed its name to Pathé Communications.

In the interim, Cannon – or rather Globus and Menahem – came up with the idea for the two Allan Quartermain films, with the dashing white hunter conducting a young woman across dangerous areas of Africa in search of her kidnapped father, leading to the mines which hold the secret of the lost treasure of King Solomon, then returning with his leading lady intact for the second adventure in which he searches for his lost brother.

The plan was to have veteran British director, J. Lee-Thompson, make the first film. The second would be directed by the less experienced Gary Nelson. Lee-Thompson was one of the great names in British cinema. Not a *great* director, but a man who had made some very fine British films in the 1950s and 1960s, such as *Yield to the Night* and *Tiger Bay*, and then made his name as an important international film-maker with the classic war epic *The Guns of Navarone*. But by the late 1970s he was in his sixties and past his best, making some of the worst of Charles Bronson's latter-day movies. When he came to direct *King Solomon's Mines*, he was 71. Ultimately, though, he still proved he had a certain flair, and the film's faults had more to do with script and production values than with Thompson's handling of it all.

Gary Nelson was a much younger but less experienced director who had made his name on TV. Among his numerous television feature films was the superior *Washington Behind Closed Doors*. His first big theatrical feature was a Disney sci-fi adventure, *The Black*

Hole, but he had done little else of note before starting his disastrous task on *Allan Quartermain and the Lost City of Gold*.

Richard Chamberlain was picked to star as Quartermain; a fine choice since Chamberlain was handsome and still sufficiently young-looking, even at the age of 50, to carry off the many acts of derring-do. He was one of the rare exceptions of a TV star who made it to the big screen, having made his name as *Dr Kildare*. His looks certainly helped him to bridge the gap between TV and film, but his greatest asset was that he genuinely was and remains a very fine actor who overcame his TV persona in a succession of period films, ranging from the controversial *The Music Lovers* to the romantic *Lady Caroline Lamb*, the swashbuckling *The Three Musketeers* and the musical fairy tale *The Slipper and the Rose*. He'd even tackled Shakespeare on film, playing Octavius in *Julius Caesar* opposite Charlton Heston's Antony. However, after his huge success back on TV in *The Thorn Birds* in 1983, he no longer seemed to fit in with the kind of action films that kept the cinema box-office tills ringing and established the likes of Harrison Ford as Indiana Jones, Sylvester Stallone as Rambo and Arnold Schwarzenegger as Conan, all larger-than-life heroes. What Cannon were after was a film in the tradition of *Raiders of the Lost Ark*, with Allan Quartermain coming out of the same mould as Indiana Jones. The script, therefore, was tailored to this end, taking extreme liberties with H. Rider Haggard's original story. For Chamberlain it was a chance to be flippant and larger than life, bringing him bang up to date with mid 1980s filmgoers.

Cannon began the search for a glamorous actress to complement Chamberlain's rugged and humorous hero. As it happened, Sharon was now with Creative Artists Agency, who had some kind of deal with Cannon Films, and they told Sharon that she should accept the role of Jesse Huston who hires Allan Quartermain to find her missing archaeologist father. CAA told her, 'We'll waive our commission because this is good for you. It's important to be *starring* in a movie.' According to Sharon, who felt that she went into it ill-advised and blinkered: 'I had an agent that sold me out.'

Later, in 1992, she was a little less bitter about the experience, and said, 'When we began making the film – or films – I was excited because I was making a big adventure movie with Doctor Kildare, for God's sake.'

Greenburg was given a job as a co-producer, so he and Sharon came as something of a package. They flew to Zimbabwe to begin filming on 6 January 1985, in Harare.

King Solomon's Mines was to be vastly different from the two previous versions. The last had been made in 1950 by MGM, with Stewart Granger as a dashing Allan Quartermain and Deborah Kerr as the woman who hires him to find her missing husband – who fortunately turns out to be dead, allowing her to fall in love with Quartermain. It was a big-budget Technicolored adventure with some impressive action scenes.

Prior to that, the story had been told in a prestigious black and white British production made in 1937. Black singer Paul Robeson starred as a native carrier who turns out to be a king, and Cedric Hardwicke was a very British, no-nonsense Allan Quartermain who is looking, not for lost husbands or father, but a lost diamond mine. Anne Lee provided the love interest, but not for Quartermain; his younger companion played by John Loder was the one who got the girl. The film boasted some excellent production standards and gave Robeson the opportunity to sing a few songs en route across Africa.

Both the earlier versions had been highly popular, but Cannon felt the time was ripe for the story to be retold Spielberg-style. The only problem was that Cannon, who were making scores of bad action movies during the 1980s and losing fortunes, couldn't afford to make it to the standard of *Raiders of the Lost Ark* and its sequel *Indiana Jones and The Temple of Doom* and *Indiana Jones and the Last Crusade*, which were all made on huge budgets. Consequently, most of Cannon's films were cut-price actioners, including their *Superman IV* which suffered from being made with less money that it needed. To make the two Allan Quartermain films back to back would help to save money, but ultimately the films were going to suffer from a lack of finance, and from being made under the most difficult conditions over a period of almost a year. It was hardly good sense whichever way you looked at it.

J. Lee-Thompson was used to shooting under tough conditions.

In 1961 he filmed *Taras Bulba* in Argentina, which doubled for sixteenth-century Ukrainian steppes. It was a big, sprawling chaotic epic that took countless months to shoot, during which Lee-Thompson was beset with all sorts of problems. Thirty-eight-year-old Tony Curtis, married to Janet Leigh, fell in love with his 18-year-old leading lady; the battle scenes featuring Argentinian cavalry and gauchos as Cossacks and Polish soldiers were difficult and dangerous to shoot; then producer Harold Hecht and United Artists pulled the plug on the production before Lee-Thompson had finished filming.

The Guns of Navarone was another tough epic in which Lee-Thompson put stars Gregory Peck, Anthony Quayle, Stanley Baker, James Darren, David Niven and Anthony Quinn into a huge tank at Shepperton Studios and blasted them with 16 tons of water from six jet spots, from which the starry cast emerged battered, bruised and cut. Then, on location in the Aegean, the special effects team set off an explosion that nearly sank a Greek patrol boat, for which producer Carl Foreman had to reimburse the Royal Hellenic Navy.

So Lee-Thompson knew all about making tough movies. He told me:

When we shot *King Solomon's Mines* in Zimbabwe, they were in the run up to the elections in what had been Rhodesia. There was political unrest everywhere. People were being abducted and murdered, and both private and commercial property burned down. Visitors to the country had been killed, so the government arranged for us to have security as they didn't want Richard Chamberlain or any of the others getting killed in their country. We felt wonderfully safe but, of course, we couldn't go anywhere, which was harder on Richard and Sharon and the other actors who were unable to see anything of the country when they weren't called.

We shot at the end of a three-year drought, and nobody had expected the drought to end. But it did, and we had the worst storms in the country's history. It rained twice a day, and it was just almost impossible for us to film anything outside, so production was constantly held up. But our two stars, Richard and Sharon, really pulled out the stops, working from very early each morning – from about five a.m. – into the evening.

It wasn't easy for any of us, but Sharon was still new to making films and she really wanted to gain from the experience in the jungle. She was really very plucky. She put up with a lot which a good many other actresses I can think of would have walked out on.

Then we had the local superstitions to deal with, which would have put other actors off completely. But Richard and Sharon rose to the challenge with admirable courage and fortitude. It turned out that our fictional Sudanese village of Tongola [built at a cost of $1 million] had been constructed on what the local extras insisted was an ancient burial ground, and they said that the storms, which had come after a three-year drought, were due to us not asking from the Spirit to build the set there. It was under water much of the time. Now, of course, we could have just laughed it off, but I said to Richard and Sharon that they should acknowledge the Spirit, not to appease it but to show respect for the people's beliefs. And they did. It didn't make the rain stop, but it made our extras feel comfortable.

Sharon's recollection of the film was, 'We seemed to spend hours at a time watching the rain, and jumping with each thunderbolt. We kept ourselves entertained during the hold-ups by holding mini regattas, making model boats from pieces of bark, and setting them adrift on the flooded set.'

Chamberlain seemed to enjoy himself – or perhaps he was very good at helping to publicize the movies. He said:

Of course, it was just a wonderful thing for me not to be so deadly serious all the time, and it seemed a perfectly good movie to be making at that time with the success of Steven Spielberg's Indiana Jones films. It's the name of the game. We had all those spy films emulating James Bond back in the sixties – some were awful, some were good. *The Man From*

Uncle TV series is now a classic. So that's what you do in movies. You try to make films that you feel the public want at a certain time, and our first film, *King Solomon's Mines*, was a big success. I wish the same could be said for the sequel. Nevertheless, people remember it still, and it certainly did a lot for Sharon Stone.

Sharon wouldn't completely agree with that assessment. She said, 'I spent a year in Africa, and that'll bring your career to a grinding halt.' Nevertheless, she learned an interesting lesson, considering how she had worked so hard to transform herself from an ugly duckling into a great beauty. In Africa she was back to being just a 'Plain Jane' again. As she noted, 'In Africa, a woman's beauty is measured by how fat she is because it shows a man can afford to feed his woman.'

The problems and pressures of filming did nothing for her marriage. 'Making those films was incredibly destructive to my marriage because we were both locked in the nightmare of making horrible movies for people who didn't give a shit what we were doing anyway.'

That overall lasting impression of making the two movies discounted the fact that J. Lee-Thompson, at the age of 71, did care. He had a long-standing reputation to uphold, and as a thorough professional he was not intent on making a film that he didn't care about. But obviously to Sharon, as the months rolled on as endlessly as the rain came down, it must have seemed that *somebody* who was in overall charge should have taken more of an interest in the nightmare she found herself in.

The film, at least, featured a strong supporting cast with Herbert Lom and John Rhys-Davies as the heavies; Rhys-Davies had also been a major supporting player in *Raiders of the Lost Ark*. Said Lee-Thompson, 'With actors like that it makes it all the easier when the film you're directing is difficult enough to do.' It was, nevertheless, a relief for him when he finished his film and returned to Elstree to supervise its post-production, leaving the sequel in the hands of Gary Nelson who also had a good cast of supporting players, including James Earl Jones, Henry Silva and Robert Donner.

With ever more responsibility placed on Michael Greenburg, the pressures on both him and Sharon increased. It became obvious to all that the sequel was going to be the lesser of the two films, and it also seemed to most that Sharon Stone was throwing around more weight than she was entitled to carry.

Said Sharon, 'At that time, I didn't know what kind of actress I wanted to be or what my abilities were. I learned my lines and gave it my best shot. People thought I was just being temperamental. I was constantly trying to push and provoke everybody to make it a good movie. My marriage was falling apart. The movie was going to be bad. I'm sure I was a bitch.'

Many thought she was, as she complained about the wardrobe, the food and the director. Out of pure vindictiveness, one of the crew urinated into a tub she was going to bath in for the film. But this was a time when she felt so insecure about her work that her neurosis manifested itself as temperament. Her final analysis of her work in both films was, 'I was a bad hairdo running through the jungle!'

Then news came in October that Rock Hudson had died. Sharon was devastated and depressed. She couldn't even come home for the funeral or to pay her last respects. The whole African experience was like a never-ending nightmare.

Chamberlain, however, had nothing but praise for Sharon, and said, 'She was completely professional and delightful. We got on rather well, despite the conditions.'

The camaraderie and the skill of J. Lee-Thompson were evident in *King Solomon's Mines* which was rushed into release that year of 1985. It was not a masterpiece, but it was a well-crafted, tongue-in-cheek movie that was just a little too camp in its humour to achieve any longevity. And although it was never going to become the blockbuster *Raiders of the Lost Ark* had been, it was reasonably successful. In it Sharon displayed her aptitude for comedy and was certainly appealing, despite what she thought of herself and her performance. The sequel had no redeeming features at all. Both Chamberlain and Stone looked bored, as though they'd been through it all before, which of course they had. Worse still, the film was really incomplete when cameras stoped rolling, and a great deal of post-production patch work had to be done on it under the supervision of Newt Arnold.

Of course, the critics disliked *King Solomon's Mines*. The *Sunday Mail* thought it was 'the cinema's equivalent to junk food'. *Variety* said:

> Cannon's remake treads heavily in the footsteps of that other great modern hero, Indiana Jones – too heavily. Where Jones was deft and graceful in moving from crisis to crisis, *King Solomon's Mines* is often clumsy with logic, making the action hopelessly cartoonish. Scenes don't resolve so much as end before they spill into the next cliff-hanger. It's an unrelenting pace with no variation that ultimately becomes tedious. Neither the camp humour nor the romance between Richard Chamberlain as the African adventurer and heroine-in-distress Sharon Stone breaks the monotony of the action.

Allan Quartermain and the Lost City of Gold was actually based on a Haggard story which had been filmed in 1977 as *King Solomon's Treasure*; that had been no better than the Cannon remake, which was so bad it was shelved until 1987. *Variety* said, 'The embarrassing screenplay jettisons Haggard's enduring fantasy and myth-making in favour of a back-of-the-envelope plot line and anachronistic jokes about Cleveland.' It was not even shown in cinemas at all in Britain, where it emerged only on video. The poor scripts of both films and their lack of money proved that at least J. Lee-Thompson, even past his prime, could make the superior of the two. Nevertheless, the films – or at least the first one – gave Sharon good exposure. She knew that she would not make the big time without doing her apprenticeship in lesser films. But there's no doubt that the difficulties of working for almost a year in Africa with ultimately poor results made her feel that she had completely wasted her time, and with good humour she said years later that if there was one bit of advice she wished someone had given her at the beginning of her career, it was, 'Don't do *King Solomon's Mines*! I mean, it's on TV more often now than *Gilligan's Island*.' But she hadn't wasted her time.

*

It may have been less painful to consider that the African experience was responsible for the break-up of her marriage. But there were more fundamental reasons why her marriage failed. She had wanted to be 'the perfect wife', but she began to realize that in trying to be the perfect wife, she was actually becoming somebody she wasn't.

She had been brought up in an environment which taught her that men were the breadwinners and the decision-makers, and that all girls should grow up and get married. 'It took me a long time to understand that being who I am is enough,' she said. 'I realized that I am not what they call "the marrying kind". I was not getting anywhere in my career and my private life was a complete and utter mess.'

Michael packed his bags and left on 26th October 1986. They had been together for just over two years; they had spent almost half of their time together making the two Allan Quartermain adventures in Africa, and there had been very little else in their life. Their separation was made official on 20th January 1987. It was all very amicable, with a sharing out of the art collection and investments.

Chuck Binder became her manager, and advised her to keep making films she was offered until finally she made the one which would make her a star. He secured her plenty of auditions for mediocre movies and TV films, but she was hardly given a second glance when she tried for major parts in major films. She wanted to play the part that Glenn Close got in *Fatal Attraction*, but didn't even get an audition.

She did, however, get *War and Remembrance* which was, at $110 million, the most expensive television one-off series ever. Officially it was called a 'mini-series', but a mini-series really only ran for about three or four episodes, the trend having been started by *Rich Man, Poor Man*. But this sequel to *The Winds of War* ran almost thirty episodes in 1987, although it had been made over a period of a year before. It had a top-line cast including Robert Mitchum, Jane Seymour, John Gielgud, Victoria

Tennant, Hart Bochner, Peter Graves, Robert Hardy as Churchill, E.G. Marshall as Eisenhower, Ralph Bellamy as Roosevelt, and Steven Berkoff as Hitler.

Mitchum was 'Pug' Henry, who takes command of a cruiser after the Japanese attack on Pearl Harbor, and develops a friendship with Victoria Tennant while his wife, played by Polly Bergen, enjoys a string of love affairs. Sharon played Janice, the well-bred, educated daughter of a prominent US senator who marries Pug's son and has an adulterous affair with a naval lieutenant, played by Barry Bostwick.

Said Bostwick, 'We were all so happy to be part of the series. Everyone had a tremendous commitment to the show. Sharon, like all of us, really felt she was involved in something important. I think Sharon felt her career was moving in the right direction.'

She said, 'It was a marvellous experience for me. One that I was proud to be part of. I think that was when I started, possibly sub-consciously, reassessing my values. But I wanted to work, so I took the movies that were available to me. I took classes and I just kept working at my craft. I really didn't know what I wanted to do at that time. I liked people like Glenn Close and Debra Winger who were really taking off around then.'

Her next film was another second-rate – possibly even third-rate – cheapie, *Police Academy 4: Citizens on Patrol*. By 1987 the three preceding films had earned half a billion dollars and had become a lucrative franchise for Warner Brothers. Said producer Paul Maslansky, 'We kept the pictures constantly good-natured, not venal, not mean-spirited. And in each one we've delivered four or five jokes people talk about – jokes like the cop who is asked to help get a cat out of a tree and responds by pulling out his Magnum .44 and shooting it down.'

Sharon did the film, she said, 'because I needed a job'. In fact she found the simple-minded – or just mindless – comedy the perfect tonic after the African films. She knew it was not going to be a breakthrough movie for her, and all the jokes had been done before. But she was delighted to find that working with twelve stand-up comedians was a joy, and she found she was engaged in conversa-tions that proved them to be 'politically astute, fun, intellectual, strange, inspirational'. Making that film, she said, changed her 'for the good – really for the good'.

Police Academy 4 was, if possible, worse than Number *3*, and was undoubtedly the final straw for Steve Guttenberg who, while acknowledging that the first in the series had made him a star, refused to appear in further sequels. He recognized that the series was past its sell-by date, but Warners still made two more (to date) without him. The critics slated the film, and some hardly bothered to review it. Maurice F. Speed, in his *1988-89 Film Review* annual, said, 'Not exactly a critics' movie. But if you appreciated the taste-less fun of *PA*s 1 to 3, you may well enjoy the latest addition to the series, which digs even lower for its laughs as it ties a series of sight-and-sound gags together with an excuse for a story.' Despite the dreadful response from the critical fraternity, it proved to be another lucrative addition to the series, but by this time they were spending less to make them so they needed less at the box office to make a profit.

There followed a supporting role in an appalling action movie, *Cold Steel*, in which Brad Davis played a cop out for revenge on the psycho who had killed his father, unaware that the psycho is also after him. Pop Star Adam Ant co-starred. The film went straight to video release in Britain in 1988.

At Christmas 1987, Sharon heard news that shook and saddened her. Richard Baker, Jnr, her former boyfriend from high school, had killed himself. He had been desolate after Sharon left him and their home town to become a model, but he had gone on to marry Brenda Moore who had three daughters and a son from a previous marriage. It was said he never really got over Sharon; whatever the truth of that, he had kept in touch with her. Characteristically he continued to be periodically moody, but he made a life for himself by becoming a licensed pilot and a partner in a successful flight training school. He moved his family to Carlisle, Ohio, but as Christmas approached he became increasingly depressed. One night he disappeared with his handgun.

The police found his station wagon in a hangar at Hook Airport in Carlisle, where Baker kept his planes. He was in his driver's seat, slumped against the window, shot in the head by his own gun.

*

Still working at her craft and still taking classes, Sharon appeared in *Above the Law* – also called *Nico*. It starred the new action man of the screen, Steven Seagal, a martial arts expert and former teacher of Aikado who came to the screen with no acting experience – but he wasn't required to act. He was, in a sense, the new Chuck Norris with a little of Arnold Schwarzenegger and Sylvester Stallone thrown in. But while he was to prove more of a high-powered star than Norris, he didn't have quite the requisite chemistry of Sly or Arnie to make it really big, although to date he has established himself as one of modern cinema's most popular screen heroes. Even at the beginning of his film career, he proved that he was not afraid to speak his mind and throw a little of his muscle about. After reading the script of *Above the Law*, he told Warner Brothers, 'The concept is great but the script is not great.' They told him, 'If you're so smart, you fix it.' He did, and delivered a new version just a few days later.

In his version, his character – CIA agent Nico Toscani – has retired after learning that the CIA had been involved in smuggling opium and keeping the war going in Vietnam. He becomes a narcotics detective and discovers that the CIA are now involved in perpetuating the wars in El Salvador, Nicaragua and Guatemala. The CIA decide to deal with him and everyone associated with him, including his wife, played by Sharon Stone.

Seagal claimed that much of the film's premise was based on his own experiences and background. Whether or not he actually ever worked for the CIA is a legend he has cleverly crafted. He said that he was recruited by the CIA in the late 1970s when he was teaching Aikado in Japan. When I asked him if he ever worked for the CIA, he replied, 'No.' But he added, 'I know a lot of people in the CIA.'

When asked pretty much the same question by Roald Rynning in *Empire*, he said, 'I won't tell you that I *was* a CIA agent, but I will tell you that I know that world very intimately.' He had also said that his 'international security' work included tracking everyone 'from murderers to missing people'.

Without wanting to devote too much space to Seagal in a book about Sharon Stone, it is worth considering that one does not generally know 'a lot of people in the CIA' unless one certainly has something to do with it. He had also claimed to have been raised as a kid on the tough streets of Brooklyn, and that he was in Japan between 1968 and 1973 studying with Morihei Uyeshiba, the founder of Aikado who died in 1969. But his own mother, Pat Seagal, said that he was raised in Fullerton in California, saying he was a 'puny kid' who suffered from asthma. And Uyeshiba's other students said they had not heard of Seagal before he became a film star. When the CIA denied that Seagal had ever been associated with them, Seagal said that since the CIA are the secret service, they can never confirm his involvement.

Whatever the whole truth, he claimed that he discovered that a high-up official in the White House had given the green light for the assassination of a US Ambassador who was attempting to incarcerate some cocaine dealers in South America. The dealers warned the US Government that if they went down, they would stop all the cocaine that was funding the Contras in Nicaragua.

With this as the inspiration for the film, Seagal and director Andy Davis were convinced that the Government would find a way to stop the film ever being shown. That didn't happen, though. Seagal was in complete control of his career and he believes, 'If I taught Sharon or anyone else I've worked with anything, it's you have to travel up the escalator fighting for control of your own destiny, your own career. If you're in control, then, if you fail, you have to blame yourself, but if someone else is in control, it's a hopeless feeling.' At that time Sharon had that hopeless feeling. Part of it was the fact that she didn't like Seagal who thought she was 'just another blonde'. She was also playing a part in a film that was mere decoration.

'I was like a big mannequin – a prop in the movies I appeared in. I felt so compressed. It was excruciating. I often got really sick in the middle of production. I just couldn't face it any more. Yet I went on because I was paying my dues, trying to be a good girl, trying to do the right thing.'

Seagal maintained that although the film was considered a 'simple action film, if you listen to what's being said, there's a lot going on'. Not too many people listened that closely, certainly not in the Government, which is perhaps why there was no reason for the film to be banned. Seagal said that when he took Stone on tour to promote the film, he was not completely surprised to see a TV news report about the CIA's involvement in drugs trafficking for the purpose of funding covert operations which were thought to be funding the Contras.

The film, shot on a modest budget, was profitable in the United States when it was released in 1988, but it was not given a theatrical release in Britain where it went straight to video: Steven Seagal was not considered a box-office draw for a British audience who had never heard of him. But the video became a popular rental in both the US and the UK, and Seagal went on to bigger and better things, including *Under Siege*, again directed by Andrew Davis who also went on to better things with the film version of *The Fugitive*. Sharon remained in virtual obscurity for just a while longer.

Even if the public didn't know who she was, the people in the business were discovering her. Warren Beatty called her agent, Paula Krammer, to ask for Sharon to meet him at his house on Mulholland Drive to discuss a film. When Paula Kramer delivered the news, Sharon said, 'I'm not going to Warren Beatty's house by myself.'

'Oh, good,' said Paula. 'I want to go too.' So they went together for what turned out to be a three-hour meeting.

Sharon found Beatty to be 'a bright, interesting, occasionally fascinating man', and said it was 'a crime that he doesn't go on screen and play a character full of life, information, savvy and wonder'. The meeting had little to do with any film. He wanted to know why she had not called back a friend of his who had been trying to get her attention. She and her best friend, Mimi Craven, were often at the On the Rox nightclub on Sunset Boulevard, where she was seen by the likes of Beatty and Jack Nicholson. Someone described only as 'a friend of Warren Beatty' had indeed tried to get her attention, and she indeed ignored it. The meeting with Beatty, she said, 'helped me learn a little more about living in Hollywood'.

There followed what was reported to be a brief and passionate affair with Jack Nicholson. When once asked if the rumours were true, she said, 'Ask Jack.' Of course, nobody asked such questions of Jack Nicholson.

Her next film was another generally mindless action film called *Action Jackson*, starring Carl Weathers, a new black star who had actually been around since the 1970s when he appeared in so-called 'blaxploitation' films *Bucktown* and *Friday Foster* before making a name for himself in the role of Apollo Creed opposite Sylvester Stallone in the first four *Rocky* films. He was now making his shot at stardom, playing Jerico 'Action' Jackson, a lawyer-turned-cop on the streets of Detroit.

Said Weathers, 'I had my own company (Stormy Weather Productions) when we were making *Action Jackson*, and I think Sharon realized then that unless you have some control in your career you're the one being controlled.'

Sharon had in fact known that for some time. She had also discovered another fact of life in Hollywood: 'I learned that in this business there is Plan A in which you become successful by living and acting with a lot of integrity. Then there's Plan B where you sell your soul to the Devil and become successful. In Hollywood Plan A and Plan B patrons mingle. Because I find it hard to distinguish one from the other, I sometimes got really burned.'

Weathers was one of the action men to whom Sharon took a liking; he was not making his way to the top using Plan B. In fact, he said she taught him a valuable lesson. 'From Sharon I learned patience – and that you just keep working. There was never any doubt in my mind that one day she was going to be in the major league.' *Action Jackson*, however, wouldn't help to put her there. It was a modest success in America, but went unscreened in the UK where it turned up only on video. *Empire*, reviewing it on its video release, said it was a 'modern-day retread of the *Shaft-Superfly* formula. Vanity replaces soul on the soundtrack, and Weathers unwisely forsakes the traditional black hero's outrageous funky threads for a smart suit. Nice explosions, and some videoworthy sex'n'violence make this passable as a time-waster.'

Trying to make it into the major league was hard going. She went up for the role of Vicki Vale in *Batman*, but lost out to Kim

Basinger, another blonde bombshell hailed as 'the new Marilyn Monroe' who'd been around as a leading lady a lot longer than Sharon and who would remain a major competitor for a few more years. Sharon also lost out to Madonna as Breathless Mahoney in *Dick Tracy*.

For years producers had been telling her, 'Baby, you're the next Jessica Lange.' But when the time came to cast her, they were somehow never quite so accommodating. She tested for a lot of films and often found that although the director and the leading star would both want her, the studio tended to put her on hold for a couple of weeks while they tried to see if they could get a bigger name. Recalling that on three such occasions the leading men called her to say, 'I just want you to know I still wish it was you', she said that these actors had not said that 'because the actress wasn't any good but because we had a particular rapport'.

For years she had also been cast as 'the pretty young thing'. But ironically she had not been allowed to exude sex in her films, so therefore she was not considered to be sexy by the studios. She recalled, 'I kept getting back "she's no leading lady".'

She was in a handful of films that went virtually unnoticed. *Tears in the Rain*, made for Showtime Cable Network, she described as 'a soppy Harlequin romance'. She recalled, 'I got such a vicious, scathing review in *Variety* that lots of big stars and producers sent me consoling letters, flowers and gifts!'

Then came – and went – the remake of the remake of *Blood and Sand* in 1989. 'I played the role that did wonders for Rita Hayworth (in the 1941 version opposite Tyrone Power) but which did considerably less for me.'

She was also in a forgettable sentimental romance called *Beyond the Stars* – also known as *Personal Choice*, made for American cable TV. Christian Slater stared as a young man who falls for the daughter of a retired astronaut, played by Martin Sheen. Sharon played the love interest, even though she was ten years older than Slater, a promising upcoming young star who had recently got himself into trouble by getting arrested for drunken driving. 'I used to subscribe to the James Dean school of thought,' he said. 'Live fast, die young and leave a good-looking corpse.'

Sharon had seen it all before, with models she'd worked with taking to drink and drugs, so she recognized the self-destructive programming Slater had himself tuned into. He was notorious also for destructive flings with the likes of Winona Ryder, Kim Walker and Patricia Arquette. He was only 20, behaving like a bad boy, and so Sharon was not going to get involved. By the time he was well into his twenties, he had lost the James Dean school of thought, saying, 'Now I'm concerned with living as long as I can and enjoying a good quality of life.'

Prior to working with Sharon, he had made a considerable impact in major roles in *The Name of the Rose* and *Heathers*, and seemed to wind up making *Beyond the Stars* as an interim while waiting to become a major star in hits like *Interview With the Vampire* and *Broken Arrow*. As *Empire* asked when reviewing it on video, 'Quite what these two accomplished actors (Slater and Sheen) are doing in this TV movie is anybody's guess, but the end result is a watchable, if somewhat predictable story of lurve and ambition.' There was no question about what Sharon Stone was doing in it, but then no one, not even *Empire*, expected her to go on to bigger things. Sharon, too, was beginning to wonder if she would do any better than this.

At least she was getting recognized occasionally, even if no one could quite remember her name. She recalled that a year after making *Action Jackson*, she was in a New York taxi cab that crashed into the cab in front, and as she jumped out to shout at the gathering crowd, 'Did anyone see what that stupid idiot did?' somebody replied, 'Weren't you the girl in *Action Jackson*?'

Time was passing and she was getting frustrated not to be doing better:

I was doing good work in not so good movies. Over the years I'd been devoted to training, studying and working. You're not going to go for brain surgery from somebody who just got their bachelor's degree. You train, learn and grow and it's natural that you move into that group of people who are doing the same thing. I *earned* my way into that club. After a certain point I became complacent. I had a job. I worked regularly. I did three pictures a year. I travelled. I bought a house. It wasn't my dream, okay. But then I went, 'I hate my life! I hate my life!'

4

From Mars to *Playboy*

In 1989 Sharon was sent a script by Carolco, one of Hollywood's most successful new independent production companies, with a memo reading, 'We're interested in meeting you for this action movie.' She angrily replied, 'I've done every stupid action movie I'm ever going to do. No thank you.'

They told her, 'But this one has Paul Verhoeven directing it.' She knew of the Dutch film director's work. Before making a splash in Holywood with *Robocop*, he had established himself in Europe with highly regarded works such as *Soldier of Orange, Turkish Delight, Spetters* and *The Fourth Man*. 'I had seen his films and thought they were terrific,' she said. She told Carolco, 'Okay, okay, I'll do it. We don't need to have a meeting. If he wants me I'll do it.' But Verhoeven did want a meeting. 'When I met him, I was completely enamoured of him,' Sharon remembered.

She also met the star of the new movie, Arnold Schwarzenegger, who was not only the star but virtually the driving force behind the whole production. He had script approval, director approval, cast approval – he was, as she would discover, the Boss, and he and Verhoeven wanted her to audition. She recalled:

They didn't want to audition me at the studio. They took me to a hotel in Los Angeles and booked into a room for *three*. The guys at the desk must have thought there was something kinky going on. Paul and Arnie told me they needed an actress who could be physical in body and mind, and Paul wanted Arnie and me to act out the bedroom scene where I get to brutalize Arnie. So I really went at him, kicking and punching him in the chest before he knew what was happening. Then he began to react and we were then in full swing. I got to look over at Paul sitting on the couch. He had this frown, and he said, 'Okay, Arnie, she'll do the job.'

The film, *Total Recall*, was a futuristic, violent, action-packed adventure, immediately superior to her previous action films by virtue of not only Verhoeven, but a huge budget – $50 million – and a huge star. Sharon's role, that of Arnie's wife with a dangerous streak to her, was, she said, 'a physical role, and I think they were looking for someone tall and athletic, and really extroverted'. She worked out for two months before beginning the film, doing circuit training. She did the Life Cycle for half an hour each day, followed by the weight machines. 'I'd move, move, move for three hours, then I'd finish with sit-ups and stretching. I worked my buns off.'

She also learned karate, which resulted in a big bruise on her jaw. When she went out to socialize, everyone thought her boyfriend had beaten her up. She recalled, 'It was the first time I got that vibe about what battered women go through.'

The film was set in the year 2084. Arnie played Quaid, a seemingly dull construction worker with a beautiful wife, played by Sharon, and an obsession to visit Mars. He is plagued by dreams about the planet in which he is with a beautiful woman. He visits Rekall Inc., a unique travel agency which implants visions of fantasy holidays which reproduce memories of vacations taken by others. The experience makes him suspect that he is really a secret agent whose memory has been erased while on a mission to save Mars from a brutal tyrant. He becomes convinced of this when his wife tries to kill him in the scene which provided Sharon with her audition.

To discover the truth, he goes to Mars and finds a beautiful woman, played by Rachel Ticotin, whom he's seen in his dreams. The film thereafter follows numerous plot twists and displays extreme violence, all skilfully woven into a slick, clever sci-fi action film.

The screenplay was based on the book *I Can Get It for You Wholesale* by *Blade Runner* author Philip K. Dick. The screen rights and the various screeenplay drafts belonged to Dino De Laurentiis, for whom Arnie had made *Conan the Barbarian, Conan the Destroyer* and *Red Sonja*. It was De Laurentiis who really made Arnie into a star. Before that he was an Austrian champion bodybuilder whose childhood hero had been Steve Reeves in Italian sword-and-sandal epics like *Hercules* and *Goliath and the Barbarians*. Schwarzenegger was, perhaps, the example of a star who, by the law of averages, should never have been one. He certainly couldn't act when he appeared briefly in the 1976 film *Stay Hungry*, and his next film, a documentary – albeit a much praised one – *Pumping Iron*, seemed hardly likely to make an actor of him. Then his lack of acting ability really came to the fore in the comedy western *Cactus Jack* opposite Kirk Douglas, in which Arnie was cast as 'Handsome Stranger' more for his physique than anything else. Above all, he had that name, although he once tried changing it to Arnold Strong, but that didn't help. He really was the man who should have faded away into obscurity.

Then Dino De Laurentiis, the often courageous and reckless Italian movie mogul who made such risky blockbusters as *War and Peace* and *The Bible in the Beginning*, cast him in *Conan and the Barbarian*, which not only kicked off the brief genre of sword-and-sorcery pictures but made Arnie into a star. The film's director, John Millus, cleverly kept Arnie's dialogue to a minimum, as did James Cameron when he cast him as *The Terminator* two years later. Schwarzenegger made two more films for De Laurentiis, and remained grateful to him for giving him the big break, and together Arnie and Dino had long planned to make *Total Recall*. But De Laurentiis's recklessness finally brought him to the verge of bankruptcy as his once considerable movie Roman empire finally crumbled. So Schwarzenegger persuaded Carolco to buy the scripts from De Laurentiis for $3 million.

Schwarzenegger himself came more expensive. He had carefully moulded his screen image as a virtually indestructible super-being whose actions were ear-piercingly louder than his words, gradually finding his own style of laconic performance and deadpan humour. By the time he came to make *Total Recall* he was not only just about the biggest star in Hollywood in every sense, he was a virtual industry around which everything else revolved. Therefore Carolco thought he was well worth the fee of $10 million they paid him, plus 15 per cent of the gross.

Said Arnie about his determination to bring *Total Recall* to the screen: 'I was interested in it because it had twists in the story that action films don't usually have. I found that I had to read right through to the last page to know what was happening, and I liked the idea of the confusion between what was a dream and what was real. I thought that audiences the whole world over would enjoy the mixture of suspense and futuristic action.'

Master of his own career, Arnie chose Paul Verhoeven to direct because, he said:

When I saw *Robocop* I thought he could be the one to do *Total Recall*, because if someone can master the combination of intense action and then make fun of the whole thing, that's really an art. A film this size needed a diector who had the mental and physical energy to keep interested right through the years it takes to get it to the screen, and who has a sense of technology for shooting special effects and using blue screen, and also of directing actors. Verhoeven is one of the few who can, along with John McTiernan and Jim Cameron.

When Verhoeven came onto the project, he read the several different drafts of the screenplay that had been commissioned. He finally chose the version that Ron Shusett and Dan O'Bannon had written back in 1985; then he brought back Shusett to rework the screenplay with Gary Goldman. Verhoeven explained,

The basic issue for Shusett and O'Bannon was a science-fiction adventure story with a very strong underpinning of the mind story. That worked for two acts. Both levels were available, there was always a strong mind-level basic to the story, while the sci-fi adventure action was on the other level. But I felt that in the third act the mind-level was lost, and Arnold agreed. What Gary Goldman did was find one basic device to include a mind-level – I would say a mind-fuck in fact, because it's about mind-fucking – and Arnold even says, 'This is the best mind-fuck yet.' Everything you have seen before is suddenly reversed and seen in a different perspective and then you realize it was all part of a bigger plan that you didn't see before – like *The Spy Who Came in from the Cold*.

Verhoeven was instrumental in transforming Arnie, whose physique can never be hidden, from the Walter Mitty-type character as originally written into a gentle giant who lacks confidence in the beginning, and is henpecked by his wife, before becoming an invincible hero.

Although Verhoeven was the director, the constant driving force behind the film was Schwarzenegger. 'If he likes the director and he thinks he is doing a good job,' said Verhoeven, 'then he supports him as I have never seen an actor do. If he puts his weight behind something, it's not just the weight of an actor, it's the weight of a politician.'

Schwarzenegger virtually co-produced the film, but in his own unofficial, offhand style. He had to step in between Ron Shusett and Paul Verhoeven when writer and director clashed over the concept of the people of Mars being suffocated by the dictator as a punishment, and their rescue by Quaid. The director wanted to take it out of the story, concerned that the audience would not buy it but find it too schmaltzy. But Arnie liked the emotional pull of the whole concept, and backed Shusett.

He was behind every decision, every detail, and Sharon was well aware of this. She said, 'He showed us what could be done. I'm not saying you have to love Arnold, but you could admire him for what he achieved.'

Filming was at the Churubusco Studios in Mexico, the only available studio with the ten sound stages the film required. It would take ten months to shoot; Sharon was needed for half that time. She said, 'I knew from Africa that on long location films, you've got to know when to make a joke and when to take a joke. I made fun of him from the start. We were rehearsing the bedroom scene in a hotel room, Arnold was lying on the bed and Paul was on top of him, straddling him, caressing his hair, explaining to me how he thought the scene ought to go. I said, "I think I'll leave you two guys alone. You're so darned cute together!" '

She also had to work hard and, as she put it, 'prove my chops to earn Arnold's respect. It was tough, and I did it – that's why I liked this part.'

When she got to Mexico she continued her fitness regime in the hotel in Mexico City. 'I'd work out until guys would puke, and then I would stop. It was kind of a macho thing for me. Before it was over I was big, I was buff. I could kick some ass! The fight scenes with Arnie were exhausting but they were a blast.'

After filming the big fight scene in which Arnie finally kills her off, saying, 'Consider that a divorce,' he showed her a huge bruise on his leg and told her, 'I've made all these action movies, I've done all that stuff in the jungles, and look! You did this to me!'

She recalled, 'I felt really big about that.'

He may have been tough in the film, but Sharon said, 'Arnold is the biggest baby you'll ever meet. Just a big, big baby. But he wants you to do the best you can because he wants his team to win. It's not an individual sport for Arnold.'

During filming Arnie's wife, Maria, arrived from Los Angeles to tell her husband he was to be a father. She recalled that when she met Sharon, she found her to be rather shy. 'She was very different from what people might think,' said Mrs Schwarzenegger. 'She made an effort to get to know me which I appeciated. There was a softness to Sharon that I think people are unaware of; they're intrigued by her image but don't know the person.'

The long location in Mexico took its toll on many of the cast and crew. 'Everybody got sick from the air pollution and the water,' said Verhoeven. 'Every day one to ten people were sick.' Verhoeven himself had difficulty sleeping and became more and more bad-tempered. 'I get so frustrated,' he said, 'then I get angry. Then I yell and scream.'

That's when Arnie would step in. He said:

Because of my positive outlook I can be helpful. I'm always there to pull things together, pour a thimbleful of schnapps, put on the Austrian music, cheer things up and keep everything on track. Paul was so close to the project that he couldn't step back. I'd sit everyone down, throw parties. I'd be on the phone at night calling Mario Kassa [Carolco chairman] saying, 'Put another million into the promotion,' calling Tristar chairman Mike Medavoy, Columbia chairman Peter Guber. I don't get paid for it. It's a great battle. A total joy.

A major contribution acknowledged by the director, the star and the writers was Rob Bottin, who devised and created the film's special effects. As a virtual youngster he had assisted Rick Baker on the cantina scene in *Star Wars*, and had gone on to work on *The Howling* – in which he developed groundbreaking effects in werewolf transformation – and *Robocop*.

Often the effects as scripted by Ron Shusett and Gary Goldman were just vaguely described, and it was left to Bottin to elaborate and create them. Said Verhoeven, 'Just from a dramatic point of view, he was extremely creative.' It was Bottin who came up with the idea of the face-splitting sequence. Commented Ron Shusett, 'The script might say "The face splits open." And then he comes up with an idea like this jigsaw puzzle which was mind-blowing when I first saw it. And the bug coming out of Quaid's nose was inspirational. Rob said, "Let's make it bigger than the nose." With the red bulb effect it turned into something fantastic instead of slimy and unpleasant.'

Bottin also collaborated with Verhoeven on devising the robotic cab driver. He designed the driver to look like a 1950s gas station attendant, with movements linked by computer to an actor so that dialogue and mouth were in synchronization.

At some point during production, someone told Sharon, 'You know, Arnold doesn't like you.' She was not so perturbed by the allegation but by the fact that nobody had asked her what she thought of him. She rang back the person and said, 'Did anyone wonder if I like Arnold, or does his opinion only count because he's a big star?'

Arnie certainly never went on record as saying he didn't like Sharon. He did say, 'It was a difficult film to make but everyone learned from it. Sharon Stone was perfect in the role and I believe that was because we all worked hard at it – Sharon, Paul and myself. Sharon knew that there were no short cuts. She had to look the part and be the part. I think that's the big lesson she learned from the movie. There were so many things going on that everyone had to pull their weight.'

She said the big lesson she learned from Arnold was, 'You get nothing for nothing. You have to work your ass off, and that's why you get success.'

Sharon finished her twenty weeks on the film; Verhoeven and Schwarzenegger still had another twenty to go. Back in California, she poured almost every cent she had into a new house that gave her a view of the entire San Fernando Valley. She could expect to do a lot more and better-paid film work, knowing that *Total Recall* was almost a surefire bet to put her further up the success ladder, so she could afford a luxury home at long last. Then, one evening, she was on her way back from an acting class, driving her BMW through the sleaziest part of Sunset Boulevard (passing a strip joint and a couple of cops picking up hookers) when suddenly a Cadillac drove head-on into her. It had come down the wrong side of the street, driven by what turned out to be an illegal immigrant.

The BMW was a write-off. Sharon staggered onto the pavement in such severe shock that she didn't realize how badly injured she was. In fact, she had a broken rib, dislocated jaw, sprained back and twisted knee. She sat on the street for ages, crying hysterically; nobody recognized her.

Eventually she managed to get home and went to bed. When she awoke in the morning she got up and tried to walk through her house but – unknowingly suffering from concussion and in considerable pain – she simply lay down on the floor and cried. She managed to get herself to the hospital and there discovered how much she had been injured. Her doctor believed that but for the training she had undergone for *Total Recall*, which had considerably strengthened her, probably she would not have been able to walk again. She later acknowledged that the quality of her life had been improved by *Total Recall*, 'saved by it really,' she said, 'and I owe that to Arnold.' She had to undergo several months of physiotherapy, and spent weeks in a back brace and a clavicle collar.

Some of the friends she had thought were among her best failed to turn up at her home to visit. She began to realize who her real friends were – that she was one of those 'life of the party girls', and now that she couldn't entertain them, they didn't want to know. The big surprise was that the friends from whom she had not expected anything were those who turned up to help her through.

She spent months after the crash at home, often alone, reflecting over her life. 'I did not feel sorry for myself,' she said. 'It made me more focused and I realized that I did not want to be working non-stop to my forties, still desperately trying to make some impact.'

Then came an invitation to a reunion at her old high school, and a request that she give the opening address. As she began writing down what she wanted to say, she realized that she had to make some changes in her life or she would never work again. She believed that she could have been killed in the crash. Now she had to decide what she was going to do. She even considered giving up acting to either study law or teach acting.

Almost the moment she arrived in Meadville for the reunion, before seeing any of her old friends, she met Richard Baker, Snr. He recalled, 'I was deeply moved that she took time out from all that was going on, from the public, to be with me. She was truly a good listener and was trying to help me.' They talked for half an hour.

In her commencement speech, she told her classmates, 'When you are in high school your success is measured by how much you are like everybody else. But from the second you graduate and on to the end of your life, it's measured by how much of an individual you are.'

Her own words made things clearer for her. She said, 'It made me realize that it was time to stop accepting things other than what was truly me.'

When she went back to Hollywood, she wrote to Richard Baker, saying:

You are the head of a large family, all of whom to varying degrees are living with this pain. Guide them. You are the head of a school, of young, hopeful students, full of life. Teach them. They too will face this point of turmoil in their lives. In whatever state he made his choice, your son made his own choice. And now, perhaps, it is best to respect that choice. For you to allow him to rest in peace means you must try to live in peace and in love with the rest of your beautiful family. And know that my thoughts, my love and my prayers are always with you. Because you, above all teachers, inspired me to live and to see.

Love, Sharon

Total Recall opened in 1990 to generally good reviews. *Variety* said, 'While the temptation is just to shrug off *Total Recall* as an excessive but exciting "no brainer", enough intelligence and artistry lie behind the numbing spectacle to also make one regret its heedless contribution to the accelerating brutality of its time.' It's ultra-violence was the very thing that raised the hackles of most critics.

Empire's Kim Newman liked it, saying, 'If you've got the stomach for the brutality, then this, ladies and gentlemen, is the first great science-fiction movie of the nineties.' She liked the way 'the film keeps pulling the narrative rug out from under you in thoroughly unexpected ways' and suggested that this was one action which 'isn't afraid to have a brain or two in its head'.

Few critics made mention of Sharon's contribution. But the film was a big, big hit, and although she was lost amongst the heroics of Arnie, the noise of machine guns, explosions and the wild, incredible special effects, she was in a huge success. 'This film made the difference after nearly twenty films and more than sixty TV commercials,' she said. 'The *Total Recall* experience did everything for me. It gave me box-office viability. Everybody knew who I was then – not that I was Sharon Stone, but that I was that girl in that hit movie. It made so much sense to move on as positively as I could from there. Anything else would just have been wasting chances.'

She had spent several months lying on her back, trying to decide what to do to boost her career before she reached her forties. She said, 'Once I realized that I had become a good actress, which I realized by working in my acting class, not by doing the terrible movies I was doing, I started to realize that in order to be a great actress and have access to great material, I needed to be a movie star. And I was so old that I was gonna have to do something fast to make it happen. So I did, you know, these publicity things.'

Among 'these publicity things' was posing nude for *Playboy*. They had been asking her for a long time but she had always resisted. At first she considered her imperfect shape unsuitable for *Playboy*, but over the years she met ten 'Playmates' and noted that not one of them had a perfect body.

In 1990 she agreed to pose. Her reason ultimately for doing it was to put her – as Sharon Stone and not 'the girl from *Total Recall*' – in the forefront. Monroe had done the same thing; so had Stella Stevens. 'I got to 32 having made so many hideous films,' she said, 'and I knew I had to do it or get out. People said my problem was I just wasn't sexy because I didn't wear tight skirts and have big hair. It was while I was recovering and doing a lot of thinking that I realized you have to have sexuality and sensuality to really make it. So I decided to do *Playboy*.'

She also considered it a stand against ageism. At 32, she was no longer regarded as a 'young pretty thing', and said, 'Women my age do not get leading roles and you need to be sexually appealing for parts in the movies you might be right for. It's a man's world and when you look like I look, that's what it is. I'd taken my top off in three movies and nobody noticed. I felt I was re-owning my femininity. I don't want to be a man, and it's not an option that I'll ever be Meryl Streep.'

She also needed the money – which she admitted – and was acutely aware of how it might affect her parents. 'I knew that living in a small town it would affect their lives,' she said, so she told them what she was going to do. 'Dad said if it would be good for my career, I should go ahead and do it. He just says that it's a fact of life that people take off their clothes, so carry on!'

The photogapher, Phillip Dixon, said, 'She was very adventurous. She suggested more risqué things than I wanted to do. Wearing nothing but high-heeled shoes and panties, she scaled a narrow fire-escape ladder, climbing forty feet. 'She was prepared to do anything to make the picture session a success,' said Dixon. One of the pictures showed her completely naked. She said, 'The photographer wanted me as I am, and that was just fine. Wet hair, no make-up, no clothes – that's just as naked as you can get.'

On the cover she was bare-breasted, sucking an ice cube. The issue is now sold out, and a collector's item. Sharon conceded that the whole exercise 'wasn't exactly subtle. It was like through the megaphone, "Hey, look at this!" '

In keeping with the tradition of quoting their models, *Playboy* quoted Sharon as saying, 'I like a man whose brain is more expansive than his penis,' and 'Sex is so much more in the mind than in the body.'

She was pleased with the final outcome and told me, 'I'm not ashamed of my body, and I did it by my own rules. I thought it was very flattering to be asked by them to do it, and I didn't see anything wrong in it. When my dad saw it he said I looked beautiful.'

Her father said, 'It didn't embarrass me any. Why should it? I thought she looked beautiful in the magazine. If it helped her career, why not? This is her life, not our lives.'

And her mother commented, 'It's a role – and we understand it's a role. Of course, our next-door neighbour might not see it in the same way we do, but we understand what she's doing.'

The spread in *Playboy*, and the success of *Total Recall*, certainly made a difference. But superstardom was still not immediate. She made a series of films in 1990 in quick succession, most of which were forgettable. *He Said, She Said* was a romantic comedy of a doomed love affair between Baltimore newsfolk, played by Kevin Bacon and Elizabeth Perkins. Sharon was further down the cast list, playing, she said, 'a blonde who was beyond all the rules – insane, nasty – and I loved it'.

It was filmed in two parts, and had two directors to helm each part: Ken Kwapsis directed the first half in which Bacon tells his story, and Marisa Silver directed the second half, which is told from

Perkins' point of view. It was certainly a good idea, with good performances. But it was let down by a script that should have been wittier, and its poor reception when released in America in 1991 meant that it went unreleased in the UK except on video.

Then came *Scissors*, in which she was billed second to Steve Railsback and reunited with Ronny Cox from *Total Recall*. It was supposedly a suspense-horror flick in which she found herself trapped alone in her apartment. *Empire* thought it was good fun and suggested it was something of

> . . . a pleasant resurrection of the sixties it's-all-a-plot plot, as used in a variety of Hammer films. This had a traumatized Sharon Stone lured to a luxurious show apartment in an unfinished building and locked in with a scissor-stabbing corpse and various automated tricks that serve to unhinge her. With an overly complicated and melodramatic plot underpinning, this relies very heavily on Stone's fragile performance and some neat directorial tricks involving such scary *objets trouvés* as a collection of antique dolls, a squawking raven and the subtly off-putting decor of the flat that becomes a prison.

Sharon's own tongue-in-cheek appraisal of the film was, 'It'll be the next *Rocky Horror Picture Show*.'

Year of the Gun offered her a more important role in a more important film, directed by an important director, John Frankenheimer. He had been a veteran of the so-called Golden Age of TV, when plays were transmitted live; he directed no fewer than 125 of those, including a number of the celebrated *Playhouse 90* series. His beginning in feature films was rather tentative, making his cinema debut in 1957 with *The Young Stranger*, a remake of a TV play he'd directed. Although it was well received, he returned to TV and didn't make his second film, *The Young Savages*, until 1961. Then, after another highly praised film, *All Fall Down*, Burt Lancaster hired him to direct *The Birdman of Alcatraz*, which firmly established him as a new leading film-maker. He went on to make scores of films, some quite brilliant like *The Manchurian Candidate* and *Seven Days in May*, some surprisingly dull like *I Walk the Line* and *The Horsemen*.

By the 1980s, he was still working but not producing work of the same calibre as his early promise. Nevertheless, he was much respected and still able to summon up the occasional extraordinary flair when attempting more thoughtful action films, like *Year of the Gun*. Sharon almost took a step back into her own past for this drama, set during 1978 in Rome at the time of the clashes between fascist groups and the Marxist Red Brigade. She played what was probably her best part so far, that of photojournalist Alison King who joins forces with young American novelist, David, played by Andrew McCarthy, in Rome to research for his planned novel: a fictional account of a Red Brigade plot to kidnap a prominent politician. In the process they discover that there actually is such a plot, and that some of David's friends are involved. They proceed to try to infiltrate the Brigade.

Frankenheimer was by far the most eminent of the directors Sharon had worked with so far – apart from Woody Allen, but that was barely a day's work – and her acting thrived under his hand, resulting in what was her best performance to date. But despite the aforementioned occasional flair of Frankenheimer's directing, the film lacked enough tension and thrills to really make it work, although it remains well worth seeing. For once Sharon was not so much a 'beautiful blonde' because Frankenheimer wanted her to look less than her usual glamorous self, and so he had cinematographer Edward R. Pressman photograph her in a way that hardened her looks, a fact she seemed totally unaware of until she saw the film at a preview. She said she had been 'photographed so ruthlessly I looked like Andrew McCarthy's mother! I leaned over to my agent and said, "Do I need a face lift? Do I? Do you know any good doctors?" '

Year of the Gun was released in 1991 and actually reached British screens early in 1992. Kim Newman, of *Empire*, wrote:

The extremely complex background is skilfully evoked, and the gradual escalation of street violence allows for some expert hand-held camera action scenes. All the characters are well drawn – even McCarthy isn't a total washout, although Stone tails off dramatically – and the plot unravels in gripping fashion. However, the last reel – which resurrects the old notion that one unarmed American wimp is a match for any number of Italian terrorists – combines the cynical with the unsatisfying, and pays off with an unfortunately hilarious talk-show coda. Nevertheless, a procovative and surprisingly worthwhile little movie.

Film Review, though, found it to be a 'lacklustre political thriller (which) doesn't thrill as it should'.

Recognizing perhaps that this was her most important movie so far, Sharon made every effort to promote it and went to the Deauville Film Festival in 1991. But audiences at that time were more easily seduced by action films like *Total Recall* than something as thoughtful as *Year of the Gun*. Consequently, few saw it on either side of the Atlantic, and it began to look as though Sharon might indeed find herself working non-stop into her forties without making an impact.

Two further inconsequential films followed. *Diary of a Hitman* had her playing a woman 'who doesn't understand that Forrest Whitaker has been hired to kill her sister, so she hits on him', as she puts it. At least she got to wear a short, dark wig, but few people went to see her looking dramatically different. Another film she made, *Where Sleeping Dogs Lie*, was little seen and didn't get released until 1992. 'I played a Hollywood agent whose client is haunted by a serial killer. Just like real life in Hollywood, basically!'

It might well have been the end for Sharon Stone. But then, in April 1991, she got a call from Paul Verhoeven.

5

An All or Nothing Roll of the Dice

In June 1990, while Sharon was getting over her injuries, posing for *Playboy* and making films that were doing her no good, Carolco bought a screenplay called *Basic Instinct*. It was by Joe Eszterhas, just about the hottest screenwriter in town, who penned *F.I.S.T.* and *Jagged Edge*. Carolco paid him $3 million for his newest and most controversial screenplay to date.

Until relatively recently screenwriters were considered by studios, producers and directors to be as disposable as Kleenex. In the days of the studio contract system, writers had to clock on and off at Warner Brothers, and then they had to work in their offices which could hardly have been an environment to encourage creativity. There is an old joke in Hollywood about the actress who was so stupid, she slept with the writer.

By the 1990s the whole attitude towards screenwriters had changed. It probably began with Shane Black, who penned *Lethal Weapon*, when he was paid a record unheard-of $1.75 million in 1991 for his script of *The Last Boy Scout*. Studios had begun to feel that if they wanted the best screenplays, they needed to pay well for the best writers. Of course, in Hollywood terms, best generally means most successful. However, a select group of screenwriters found themselves in the enviable position of being able to demand enormous amounts of money. Among them was Joe Eszterhas.

During the negotiating process with Carolco, his power was such that he not only arranged the massive $3 million payment but also succeeded in getting his friend Irwin Winkler in as producer with a fee of $1 million. Winkler was no slouch when it came to producing first-class films; he had been behind *They Shoot Horses, Don't They?, New York, New York, Rocky* (and *Rocky II*) and *Raging Bull*.

The story centred around Nick Curran, a San Francisco detective with a murky past and an unfortunate ability to get innocent bystanders killed. Despite an uncertain future, he is assigned to investigate the death of a rock star, and the clues lead him to bisexual novelist Catherine Tramell. A seductively intriguing and dangerously manipulative woman, she sleeps with the prototypes of the characters she writes about so that she can get to grips with their innermost feelings and motivations. She has a lesbian lover, Roxy, who is insanely jealous; she too becomes a suspect. To complicate his investigation, Nick discovers that Beth Gardner, the police therapist he has become involved with, also appears to have a motive.

The murder proves to be just one in a string of killings. The victims are all men, killed with ice-picks while in the throes of lovemaking. As Nick finds himself drawn ever deeper into the physical and mental mind games played by Catherine, his own basic instincts come to the surface and threaten to cloud his investigative abilities before he discovers that she is the killer. 'The film is a gigantic mind game that extends into the bedroom,' said Eszterhas. 'It's a strange and twisted love story about homicidal impulse.'

He and Winkler worked closely on putting the production together, and chose their director carefully. *Total Recall* had become a massive hit, and since Paul Verhoeven was just about the hottest director in Hollywood at the time, it seemed a good idea to get him interested. He read the script, liked it and agreed to do it for $5 million. But he had reservations which he only outlined to the producer and writer after he had signed his contract.

The film had plenty of sexual content, but Verhoeven wanted to make it much stronger, much more explicit, and even had the idea of defying the censors and showing a male erection for the first time in mainstream film. But almost immediately the producer and writer made it clear that they did not want the script changed for any reason. The battle lines were being drawn up. As far as they were concerned, Verhoeven was trying to change it into a pornographic film, whereas they had 'an erotic thriller' in mind.

In October, Michael Douglas signed to play Nick Curran for a massive $15 million. By this time Douglas was one of the biggest stars in Hollywood, especially after the success of films like *Romancing the Stone* and *Fatal Attraction*. He had also proved himself to be an actor of considerable performance power with *Wall Street*. There had been a time when he was always described as 'the son of Kirk Douglas'. By this time the media had turned it around, and Kirk was being described as 'the father of Michael Douglas'. Although Michael had started his career as an actor in a couple of modest feature films and then the TV series *The Streets of San Francisco*, he had established himself in cinema as a producer with *One Flew Over the Cuckoo's Nest*.

Just prior to *Basic Instinct* his career had suddenly hit the skids when he appeared in the Second World War adventure *Shining Through*, which was savagely attacked by the critics and boycotted by the public. *Basic Instinct* came along at just the right moment for him. He said he chose to do the film because, 'I was looking to do a sexy role, and that was the initial attraction.' He explained:

Whenever I'd look at these lists of the year's ten sexiest actors, I'd never see my name on it. But perhaps that's because I'm more of a character actor. After *Shining Through* I decided I wanted to do something sexy. When I read the script of *Basic Instinct* I thought I saw it as being a sexy, psychological thriller, what I called a *Fatal Attraction* for the nineties. It was like the sort of detective novels you'd read in bed; it was stimulating but not smutty.

I was also intrigued by this guy's past. His wife has committed suicide and he's accidentally killed four tourists, and now he is getting therapy. He is struggling to discover if he has any worth at all. Then he meets Catherine who he finds is an addictive personality, and she takes him over and leads him to his dark side, his own basic instincts which are founded in sex and violence. So the film shows this struggle he has between his responsibility as a police officer and his basic instincts.

Nick has a hot temper and jumps emotionally when he shouldn't. I thought of Nick as being like a volcano that could go off at any moment. I liked the idea of playing a character with an edge, even though this is a time when we like to see our heroes as heroes. There was a time when films had anti-heroes. I find myself still intrigued by grey areas in people, especially in heroes. He has a destructive sense for danger, for sex, for drugs and alcohol.

Douglas was prepared to appear naked in what were obviously going to be heavily simulated sex scenes, but he stipulated that he would not appear full-frontal. He said, 'I didn't want to embarrass my family in that way. And I did not think the film called for those kind of shots. We all agreed that, but I asked for the clause in the contract just to make sure.' While the director struggled with his producer and writer over the script changes he wanted to make, Douglas voiced his own concerns that his character was too weak compared with the stronger role of Catherine. He also wanted to know who was going to play Catherine. His first choice was Isabelle Adjani, and because he was an extremely powerful figure who was given considerable clout on this production, the script was duly sent to her. But she was uncomfortable about the heavy sexual content and rejected it.

Verhoeven said that when he first read the script he felt that because it involved a lot of heterosexual sex, it needed some lesbian and homosexual sex to 'balance that'. He outlined all this to Eszterhas and Winkler – 'not in the nicest way probably', said Verhoeven – and outraged them. The producer said that Verhoeven had no idea what the script was really about 'and he was solely interested in how much nudity he could get from the actors – how much skin they could show'.

Producer and writer made an offer to Carolco to buy back the script, but the company backed Verhoeven and allowed Eszterhas and Winkler to walk away with their fees. Verhoeven was happy to carry on without them, and Carolco brought in highly experienced producer Alan Marshall, who had worked on most of Alan Parker's films, to replace Winkler. In December, Verhoeven brought in Gary Goldman to write his new version, which included an explicit lesbian sex scene. But he finally came to the conclusion that he had been wrong in trying to make the film even more sexually excessive – and he was prepared to admit it.

'The lesbian scene never worked,' admitted Verhoeven. 'It was just stupid, so we simply changed a few lines to make Michael's character stronger and we sent it over to Joe and he *loved* the script.' He explained that the script wasn't really about lesbians and to add more lesbian scenes didn't work dramatically. He said that from the outset he did not see what he described as 'the basement of this building', but later discovered that 'this basement was the heart of the script and it would be foolish to build the wrong building on top of that'.

Goldman's second draft was the furthest from Eszterhas's screenplay, but by the fifth draft it was becoming more like the original script. In March 1991, Carolco sent Eszterhas a copy of the final script revison. He said, 'I was flabbergasted. There were maybe half a dozen, a dozen line changes, no plot points, no character changes, just some visual changes that Paul had brought in.'

There followed a very public reconciliation between director and writer. 'We all made up in the papers to show everybody that it was just a big misunderstanding. And it *was*. I was really wrong, and I have acknowledged that my proposal was really stupid and childlike.'

With Alan Marshall now producing, the work went smoothly ahead. Then the Gay and Lesbian Alliance Against Defamation – GLAD – got to hear about it. The basic story line had become public knowledge because of the behind-the-scenes battles, and GLAD was joined by Queer Nation and other militant gay lobbyists who protested to Verhoeven over the depiction of a bisexual woman as a serial killer. They called the film 'homophobic' and 'misogynistic'.

Verhoeven got on with trying to get the film ready to roll in May

1991. But first he had to find an actress to play Catherine. Numerous star names had been approached. Verhoeven wanted Geena Davis for the role, but she turned it down. She explained:

> So many women come up to me and say how much they loved *Thelma and Louise*, that it has changed their lives. Ninety-nine per cent of movies are about women either having shallow, one-dimensional caricature parts or they're being murdered or raped. I'm interested in playing strong characters – women who get to do things and who challenge themselves and are in charge of their lives. I want to be involved in the action or have something interesting going on, not only be required to be sexy or set dressing or the victim. *Basic Instinct* isn't my idea of a juicy role for a woman. I won't make movies that women feel violated through seeing them.

Among others who were approached, and who rejected it, were Greta Scacchi, Julia Roberts, Debra Winger, Ellen Barkin, Lena Olin and Michelle Pfeiffer.

In April, Verhoeven decided to try for Sharon Stone. She recalled, 'He called me up and said, "I've got the perfect part for you." I said, "Oh Yeah!" He said, "Yeah. It's a beautiful bisexual novelist who uses her plots as the basis of a series of pattern murders." At first I was stunned. Then he sent me the script, and I was rooted. I fell for the story and the character as soon as I saw the script. I wasn't afraid of doing sex scenes that were raw, hard and violent because that's what the movie called for.'

When Verhoeven suggested Sharon for the part, Douglas was horrified because he did not consider her to be a leading actress with a proved track record. He told Verhoeven, 'I'm out there, and I'm not risking myself with some *amateur*!'

Verhoeven persuaded Douglas to give Sharon a test. As he said:

> I knew Sharon from *Total Recall* and she had these qualities in her already. But I, and Michael to a certain extent, had to be attracted to her in a romantic and erotic way to be able to shoot the film in an erotic way. If I did not like her personally,

it would be impossible to make it work. There was a kind of attraction between Michael and Sharon too, just enough to make it work, although there were no deeper elements happening there – it was all performance. Michael told me he could see enough in Sharon's eyes to make it work.

Sharon said, 'I had met Michael on two or three occasions before I tested with him for the movie. I really felt he and I could have a certain strange, dynamic energy together. I was never comfortable around him and I don't think he was comfortable around me. But our energy together was strong.'

Douglas had to admit later that his initial response to Verhoeven's suggestion of casting her was wrong. 'This movie will make her a star. She's now A-list competition for any actress in the world.'

Sharon got the part for less than half a million dollars. The fact that Catherine was bisexual didn't bother her and had clearly bothered some of the other contenders who turned it down. She knew it was going to be explicit, but she also knew that this could be the film to make her into a big star. She said, perhaps too bluntly, 'The girls who turned down *Basic Instinct* were stupid. I wanted the part badly. When I got the role, I thought, "This is the opportunity of a lifetime. I'm either gonna play this part and rock things or hang my head in shame at the supermarket." It was an all-or-nothing roll of the dice. I knew doing the film could be a risk. If it didn't work it could have ended my career completely.' She recalled that she just smiled to herself and thought, 'Okay, if we pull this off, you ladies who turned down the role will have only created more competition for yourselves!'

But she later admitted that she understood why the other actresses turned it down; they probably knew, she said, that they would eventually have to face the music over all the sensationalism the film would ultimately create. But for her it was a matter of making the most of a golden opportunity, or know that she could miss the boat altogether. 'I just wanted to play parts that didn't make me feel like throwing up or make me wonder, "What led this woman to her lobotomy?" Time was running out and I needed to be a *movie star*.'

The role itself appealed to her. 'It's so rare that a female character is more than an appendage to some guy. But I never thought of
Catherine as bisexual, or even sexual. Sex is just the currency she
uses to get what she wants. Catherine is so raw and willing to go
anywhere to pull Nick into her web. She'll seduce him in her mind.
She'll seduce him with her sexuality. And when she sees that something gets him, it makes her all the more excited.'

She felt at least that in going into an erotic movie, she was in the
hands of a director she knew and trusted. 'I don't know how far I
would go on-screen with Paul as director. I trust him a lot. But that
scares me a little. I think you have to be in control as an actor. But,
with Paul, you tend to give him the reins and say, "lead the way".'

Said Verhoeven:

As the director, I was in this triangle between Michael and
Sharon, and this psychological and sexual attraction is essential on set. I have a love-hate relationship with Sharon which
developed on *Total Recall*. She once said, 'He loves me and I
hate him.' That's not true. It's a relationship where we have
love for each other. I had big fights with Sharon but we made
up all the time, there was a lot of hugging and kissing on the
set.

We push each other's buttons. There's a lot of erotic tension
between us. But if you give this sexuality a chance you lose
control. If you are going to consummate this 'sexual' relationship with an actress, it won't work on screen any more: it cannot end up in bed with the director.

Even before filming began, there was much comment about the gay
community's growing uneasiness over the film. There was talk of
protests being organized by militant groups. In anticipation of the
troubles ahead, Michael Douglas said to Joe Eszterhas, 'Look, this
is brewing. Do you have a problem with it?'

'No,' Eszterhas replied, adding, 'I believe in every group there is
deviant behaviour.'

While they were rehearsing in San Francisco, Douglas asked
Eszterhas the same question. The writer replied, 'No, absolutely not.'

'Good,' said Douglas, 'because we need your support.'

That May the cameras began rolling in San Francisco. Almost from the beginning, the film's locations became the scenes of protests by gay groups. Richard Jennings of GLAD complained, 'The characters embody all the stereotypes about lesbians.' Queer Nation's spokesperson Judy Sisneros accused the film of adding to 'the overwhelming negative portrayal of gays and lesbians in movies, with its psychological profiles of lesbians and bi-sexual women as evil, diabolical'.

Militants besieged a country-and-western bar called Rawhide II, owned by a leading gay activist, where scenes were being filmed. They also sent the owner death threats, and Queer Nation supporters wrecked his Mercedes.

When scenes were shot at the Tosca Café, gay activists waved banners that read 'STOP!' 'HATE!' and 'HOLLYWOOD GREED KILLS', and they chanted, 'Michael Douglas, racist, sexist, anti-gay! Michael Douglas, fuck you!'

Douglas said, 'I expected some protesting to go on but not *that* much. I haven't yet talked to many people who have found a real justified reason for the militant gays and lesbians getting so upset. In movies someone's got to be the villain and it can't always be the Italians.'

Sharon actually found herself sympathetic to the protesters, saying, 'I think *Basic Instinct* really does portray these women in a very negative way. But I also think that every story has an antagonist and a protagonist and there're only two genders to pick from, so what the fuck?' She had always mixed with gays, particularly during her days as a model, and she had often gone out on double dates – Sharon and a man friend, and a gay couple. She had no fight to pick with the gay community, she was sensitive to their issues, but her 'perspective of the lesbian relationship in the film was that it was a pure loving relationship. At the same time Catherine was clearly not a lesbian, but a party girl.'

She said she understood that the gay community were using this unique opportunity as a way to be heard. 'That was good. I'm enormously sympathetic with the issue that was raised, because I know that the focus is always on the blonde people in movies.' She was sympathetic, she said, to all minority groups:

> Even though women are not a minority, we are treated like
> one. So many female characters are written the way men expe-
> rience women or would like to experience women, and that's
> not the way women really are. How often do you go to a movie
> and see a female character who is like a woman you actually
> know? I think *Basic Instinct* showed both men and women in
> the trenches pitted against one another. I sympathized with
> the protesters on this but I think you have to put the whole
> situation into perspective. This film is a psychological thriller,
> and the main emphasis is on this character that I play. She's a
> best-selling novelist who has deep psychological and sexual
> defects which affect her mental stability. It is as crucial to the
> story as the fixation with his mother that Norman Bates had
> in *Psycho*. If he didn't have that fixation and he just killed for
> no apparent reason, it wouldn't make much of a story.
>
> The homosexual or bisexual element in *Basic Instinct* is the
> motive for the killings, but it's only a *movie*. I mean, we were
> not saying that all gays and lesbians are killers. It's just a dif-
> ferent slant, and I think it makes it different and interesting.

She also said, 'I respect their right to freedom of speech. But they
should also respect my feedom of expression as an artist.'

Verhoeven was more characteristically blunt about his point of
view. 'Moviemaking is not about politically correct people. Fuck
politically correct. If there is no character that is bad, there is no
drama.'

As the cast and crew stood steadfast against the alarming growing politically correct assault on them, Joe Eszterhas, Alan
Marshall and Paul Verhoeven agreed to meet with members of
GLAD and Queer Nation in June. The activists recommended that
Michael Douglas's character be made into a lesbian, to be played
perhaps by Kathleen Turner, and that the lesbian killer should also
murder a couple of women as well as men.

It seemed clear that there would not be a merging of minds, but
to Verhoeven's complete surprise and the delight of the gay

community, Eszterhas suddenly announced that the script *was* insensitive and he was going to change it according to the activists' demands. He would also turn Curran's partner into a narrow-minded bigot who would say negative things about gays so that the lesbian detective could put him right with lines like, 'The best people in town are gay.'

Verhoeven was outraged. He said, 'We heard dialogue like that in Europe in the 1930s with "my best friend is a Jew", and you just know the people who use that line have done the worst.'

Michael Douglas was equally outraged. According to Alan Lawson in his biography of Douglas, the star said, 'Look, it's a hot, sexy thriller. That's why I wanted to do it. Joe claimed it was a matter of principle, and we now know this man has no principles.'

In Eszterhas's defence, he was understandably concerned about the extent to which the militants might go and, with a wife and children to consider, it would seem most likely that he was placating the gay community for the sake of his own family's safety. Nevertheless, star, producer and director felt betrayed by their writer, and the usually diplomatic Douglas said, 'Joe stabbed Alan Marshall in the back. I can understand that he was nervous about what the activists might do to his wife and kids, but he should have called Alan and told him in advance, instead of just blurting it out in the meeting.'

Peter Hoffman, chief executive of Carolco, joined in the attack on Eszterhas and made his feelings very clear: 'I consider his changes patronizing drivel. Joe Eszterhas is a snivelling hypocrite and I have no use for him. Besides, we would never change a script in response to political pressure.'

Artistic and creative ethics aside, the fact was that the film was half-way through shooting, and there was no way Carolco would agree to stop in mid-production, and start again. Nor was Michael Douglas likely to abdicate his role.

Once again Joe Eszterhas was out of the production, and probably relieved to be. The gay community considered him a hero; but it did nothing to change the way the film was going. When news reached GLAD and the other activists that Eszterhas's new script had been rejected, the protests became increasingly dangerous.

Fifty San Francisco policemen were called in, wearing riot gear. Sets were paint-bombed, and Douglas, Sharon and Verhoeven were often escorted from the sets into waiting cars by guards. Alan Marshall personally made 31 citizen's arrests.

At least there was peace at the palatial house in the exclusive beachside community of Stinson near San Francisco, where the scenes in Catherine's house were shot. Production designer Terence March was able to furnish the house as he needed because the owner had fallen on hard times and had sold everything, leaving an empty but beautiful cliff-top shell. March brought in valuable paintings and sculptures from well-known San Francisco artists, spending in the region of $1 million on interior decoration which, the producer agreed, was a bargain for what they had.

It was there that most of the sex scenes between Douglas and Stone were filmed. Sharon said that she wanted these to be shot explicitly in a 'raw, hard' way. 'Too many Hollywood sex scenes are so soft,' she said. 'I didn't want to do anything like that. I told the producers that if they sprayed me with water and shot me in a hazy blue light, I wouldn't do the scenes because I consider that tacky.' Verhoeven purposely avoided shooting any of these scenes during the first seven weeks of production, but he made a point of discussing them with Douglas and Sharon at least once a week. He said, 'Going on the set was like executing choreography; it was all storyboarded meticulously.'

Well aware that Carolco wanted an R rating as opposed to the harder NC-17 rating (reserved for hard porn), Verhoeven shot the sex scenes from different angles so that he could produce different versions for different markets, knowing all the time that he would succeed in getting the hardest version released in Europe. As a director, he had to find ways to photograph what was worded very simply on paper. In the script it said, 'He goes down on her.' Verhoeven said, 'I thought I could go a bit further from what he wrote but I still had a storyboard for every move, every frame, showing exactly Michael's mouth sucking Sharon's tit.'

The scenes were so explicit that the question rose later as to whether or not the two principal stars used body doubles for the more intimate parts. Said Sharon, 'It's definitely us. It's not body doubles. We did everything but anal intercourse and I don't know why that wasn't in there because, with so much violence in the characters' sexuality, that absence seems odd. Michael and I went as far as anyone could go.'

That settled, the next question people were asking was, did they actually do it for real? Explained Sharon, 'Look, I have a four-minute sex scene with Michael Douglas in which I have three orgasms. What does that tell you? Do you know woman who have orgasms from these anatomically impossible positions? In two minutes? Please! Send them over to my house so I can learn. Michael Douglas and I went as far as anyone can go. I didn't know how they'd ever get a censorship rating.'

Michael Douglas made it clear that no real sex actually went on, despite rumours to the opposite. He said:

> Making love is the act of losing control, losing yourself. But acting making love is choreographed. When she scratches your back, you have to arch two beats, three, then roll over, boom – that's what acting's about, making it totally believable, and simultaneously being aware of the moves and the technical aspects. Quite honestly, after the first ten or fifteen minutes of awkwardness, it's just marathon running. You have to be in great shape, because it's five or six days of the most exhausting scenes you could possibly do. It's not a turn-on at all.'

In the film, Jeanne Tripplehorn played the police psychologist who becomes the object of Nick Curran's lust, and in one scene he attacks her, resulting in a scene that some have labelled as date rape. Douglas outlined the way it was filmed:

> The aggressiveness of it had us both nervous. I was initiating the action and she went along. She's a great reactor and it went really well.
>
> Shooting sex scenes is like shooting a ballet. A good example is the way we filmed the rather rough sex scene between myself and Jeanne. We rehearsed it over and over, starting

slow, going through each movement, then picking up speed until it was boom, *up against the wall, kiss, kiss, kiss, boom, her leg comes up, kiss, rip open her blouse, kiss, go for her breasts, then we turn around, her back against the wall, arms up, kiss,* and you do that for twelve hours a day, five days a week, which I can tell you is *not* sexy but it is very hard work. In the end, after doing it over and over for different angles, you just want it to be over so you can go home.

Remarked Jeanne Tripplehorn, 'It was like a rodeo!'

Sharon said that shooting the sex scenes was so repetitious that 'in the end it was boring'. Nevertheless, the intimacy of the scenes between Douglas and Stone required them at least to have a rapport to make it all work. He said of her, 'I do think of her as a professional athlete. She's got kind of a jock mentality and a professional athlete's discipline. I wouldn't call her inherently sexy – though she's a beautiful woman – but she certainly uses her sexuality, among her other skills, much like an athlete might use his different moves.'

Of her relationship with him, she said, 'Our energy together was strong. It was a primal thing for me. It was all about watching him, observing his movement, provoking him. If one were to believe in karma, I would say there is some karmic circle yet unfilled between the two of us.'

She said that he was very protective towards her during the filming of the sex scenes:

We would be naked, pretending to make love, and the moment the scene was over he would be offering me a robe. When we came to shoot particular scenes which could have been embarrassing, he made jokes. Not rude jokes, just funny. He was able to stay warm that way and make me feel relaxed. I mean, he was there, exposed and vulnerable, just like I was. In the end we were so comfortable together that I could just slip off my robe and accept that I was nude.

Michael was very professional. A lot of the really hot scenes could be very embarrassing for any actor, but he was totally into it and really great. It helped, of course, that he's a very sexy man. I made love to him for a whole week on set in every conceivable position. The sex scenes were, in fact, the least spontaneous scenes from the whole movie.

She, too, was sympathetic towards Michael's own difficulties during these scenes and said, 'I wouldn't really like to be in any guy's position during movie sex scenes. You have to be so cool about things.'

In typical self-deprecating humour, she commented that on seeing the playbacks of the nude scenes, she occasionally got a shock. 'I never knew my ass was *this* wide. Why didn't somebody *tell* me? I told the cameraman, "If my legs look like this on film, I'm going to *kill* you." '

Although Verhoeven had wanted to show an actual male erection, not only was this something that would never get past the censor, but Michael Douglas was not willing to allow himself to be seen full frontal, aroused or otherwise. Said Sharon, 'I had heard when we started that he was going to let it all hang out, as they say. He does show his butt although the shots are rather coy. To me it would have been totally appropriate for Michael to be nude. But I think that's his prerogative and it's up to him to run his career the way he wants to.'

Despite all the clinical and technical approach to filming these scenes, Paul Verhoeven made a confession. 'There were a couple of moments when I was making the movie that you could feel an erection. I think it happened once or twice when I was watching Jeanne Tripplehorn and one or two times scenes with Michael or Sharon, that I felt it was highly erotic. It's not so that the crew cannot walk around any more because they all have erections, but there might be a moment where you have to sit down for a few seconds before you get up!'

Verhoeven, of course, has a very European view of sex on screen. 'You look at other cultures and you see cultures where people are just putting the penis right into the vagina. But we have this burden of thinking that sex is something you cannot show.'

He was also aware of the concerns that Michael Douglas in

particular may have had, although Douglas had made no admission to feeling that way. Said Verhoeven:

> I have this theory that a male actor has no experience of how other men are in bed. You are not aware of how they breathe, how they moan, how they move, how they start doing it, how they put it in, how they take it out, what positions they like. All of which makes you even more vulnerable because when the director's commenting on your behaviour, he's not only commenting on your acting, he's also commenting on *you*. So you think, 'Is what I'm doing, and what I do in bed with my own wife, mistress, whatever, is that not ridiculous now that I'm doing it here for 40 million people? Will I look stupid? Is my moaning and groaning too much? How would other men do it? So you have to get over that.

The most controversial scene was the one that simply became known as 'the flash' – when Catherine, in a room full of policemen who interrogate her, crosses her legs and reveals that she is not wearing any panties. She discussed the scene at length with Verhoeven and she felt confident that not only would it be right in the context of the film, it would be lit in such a way that nothing would really be seen, even though it would be obvious that she was not wearing briefs. So she agreed to do it.

She also had to film an erotic scene with Leilani Sareilli, who played Roxy, and said of it, 'I am living inside the character, so I have to think it is not *me* doing those scenes. Anyway, the lesbian love affair is the most genuinely loving in the whole movie.' She and Leilani talked at length about their scenes, and they agreed that 'love is love, whether it is between a man and a woman or two women.' Said Sharon, 'If love is between two women, what's the big deal? I wanted to do a scene that wasn't a sick male fantasy. I wanted a scene that showed two people who were crazy about each other.'

If anything in the film was at all difficult for her, it was acting out the horrific murders. In fact, they proved to be so traumatic that she had nightmares and even walked in her sleep. On the set, she would go through the motions of pretending to kill men with ice-picks while in the throes of orgasm, and then almost faint. Lying on the floor, she'd be given oxygen, and often her friend Mimi Craven would lie next to her just to talk her through it as she cried. Through her tears, she fought with Verhoeven, and the women on the set would form a pack around her to keep the director at bay, warning him, 'Don't you get *near* her!'

'It was the most *horrifying* experience,' said Sharon. She became frustrated in ensuing interviews when journalists and broadcasters continually asked her what it was like to take her clothes off. In all the interviews she did, not one single person asked her how it felt to act out taking another human being's life. 'Not *one* person,' she emphasized. 'And I have done hundreds of interviews. It's like, "Excuse me, you're sitting there judging me on whether or not I took off my clothes or had an orgasm. Why don't you look at yourself and wonder why it doesn't bother you that I stab somebody thirty-five times. How about *that* as something to deal with?" '

Playing Catherine was gruelling for Sharon. 'The character was hard to play because she is relentless at every second.' Also, the protests by gay militant groups had put extra pressure on all the cast and crew. But even away from the gay protests, filming was not all plain sailing. As Verhoeven admitted, 'I have such a strong vision that when people deviate from it I get upset or irritated.'

Sharon commented (as he had recalled) that she and Verhoeven had a 'love-hate relationship. He loves me and I hate him!'

Douglas criticized Verhoeven for never voicing his approval or disapproval, so the actor never knew how good or bad he actually was until he saw the film. 'Paul never told me how I was going. He never said a word. I don't go to see the dailies, and he just never talks.' Ultimately, Douglas was impressed enough to say, 'I'd make another movie with Paul in a second. I think he's very, very talented. God forbid you'd go through a process like that with someone who's not!'

Filming was finally completed in September, after 89 days of shooting. Its cost was $43 million. Sharon would not be needed except for some post-synching and, later, to join Michael Douglas in promoting it. Paul Verhoeven retreated into the cutting room to work on the editing and post-production. In February 1992, he produced a version that was the strongest and which he knew in his heart would only get shown in Europe. He was right. To gain the required 17 rating, he had to cut 42 seconds, mostly from the oral sex scene with 'Michael between Sharon's legs and licking and sucking and all that stuff', as put by Verhoeven. 'In the American version, you know where he is but you don't see *exactly* where, and in my favourite version, you know *exactly* where he is and what he's doing.'

6

Basic Stardom

Now that she was very much in the public eye with the protests making news, and the steamy sex scenes making headlines even before they were seen by the public, rumours about Sharon's so-called wild life – from her supposed sexual antics to alleged drug-taking – began circulating. From the day I got *Basic Instinct* I heard all the rumours,' she said. 'The drugs one was new to me! I'd just like to know how I could be on drugs and making four movies a year, because in those days I would have been doing that. I'm sure making *Police Academy 4* would have been a lot funnier on drugs.'

There were rumours that she really was gay. She said, 'I've never had sex with a woman, but I've been on dates with women. I'm not intentionally a tease. A gay woman asked me out on a date and I've gone out on a date to see if . . .' She admitted that she had been curious about lesbianism. 'Because, you know, men can be annoying. So once in a while you hope – oh God – maybe there could be an alternative. But unfortunately for me there isn't. I love women. I love being with girl friends. God! If I could get into it, it would be great. But, you know, it don't mean a thing if it ain't got that *schwing*!'

As to the rumours that she slept her way to the top, she said, 'When I did *Year of the Gun*, I heard I was sleeping with John

Frankenheimer. When I was tested for *Basic Instinct,* I was sleeping with Paul Verhoeven and having an affair with Michael Douglas. I must be *legendary* in bed. Guess it must be the drugs!'

She had learned over the years that being blonde and beautiful meant that the 'minds of Hollywood' looked upon her as a bimbo, as a 'Barbie doll', and therefore she was incapable of becoming successful by any other means than sleeping her way to stardom. 'If you are a woman finding any degree of success, that you could have possibly earned it by professionalism and integrity seems to have escaped the "minds" in this Hollywood environment.'

It came as a shock to those 'minds' to discover that Sharon had a considerable brain, a driving ambition, and a strong sense of her own femininity. She was not surprised that there were some people doing their best to put her in her place. She said, 'If you have a vagina *and* an attitude in this town, then that's a lethal combination.'

That was a line better than any screenwriter's invention. On a more basic level, she said, 'The trouble with men in Hollywood is that you can be tall, blonde and pretty – but you can't be smart. I just want to go on proving them wrong.' Some suggested she was too prone to putting her foot in her mouth every time she opened it, and she certainly failed to endear herself to many of the men who ran Hollywood. If for no other reason, her criticisms of male chauvinism, however justified, should have been enough to prevent her from going any further in her film career. The fact that she did manage to progress says more about her determination and ambition than about the men she berated.

She also discovered the horrific side to being famous. She had a frightening experience once when returning by plane to Los Angeles after a trip out of town with her friend Mimi Craven. They had arranged for a limousine to pick them up, and when they got off the plane, Sharon was feeling so exhausted that she got in the car on her own while Mimi went with the driver to get the luggage. The next thing Sharon knew, a flashbulb went off in her face. Then a man with a camera jumped into the front seat and was leaning over taking picture after picture, each time with a blinding flash.

Sharon freaked, yelling, 'Oh, my God, there's somebody in my car!' Pulling herself together she then began screaming. 'Get this asshole out of my car!'

Mimi heard her voice and came running to the rescue, diving into the car and onto the photographer. Sharon cried, 'Oh, my God, he's going to kill her.' She grabbed Mimi and pulled her down while the photographer took shots of them huddled on the floor of the car; then he fled.

For months after, the girls waited to see if the pictures would appear in some tacky tabloid with accompanying text that revealed some perverse and sordid tale of a lesbian romp; nothing materialized. But from that lesson Sharon learned that she should never travel under her own name again, since it was easy for photojournalists to check such things as flight registers and discover which famous faces worth snapping would be turning up.

What nobody knew about Sharon at that time, was that she had begun to take a secret interest in the plight of abused girls. She started visiting a Los Angeles hostel for victims, and took to working as a volunteer.

She also found time to have a boyfriend, country singing star Dwight Yoakim. Considering the impact that Sharon had been making in the media as a sizzling sexy screen star even before *Basic Instinct* was seen, it was not exactly the perfect match since he was, in her words, 'a bit of a prude sometimes'.

She had been inactive in her romantic life for some years, too busy to devote herself to anyone else in her final bid for stardom, although she would become very romantically active in ensuing years having made the grade as a star. But her character in *Basic Instinct* in no way reflected her real life, and she was known to be someone who was not 'easy' in Hollywood, which remained one of her great strengths. Nor was she a perfect angel. There were rumours of a brief fling with a millionaire playboy who flew her to Paris for a weekend in return for buying her the latest French fashions. If true – and there's no evidence that it is – it illustrates her own sense of power over men rather than the reverse.

So the woman who attracted Dwight Yoakim was not a super sex siren but an incredibly bright and beautiful woman with a quick and often wicked sense of humour. As she said, 'If you don't have a

sense of humour in this town, you can't really survive here – or anywhere. Life will just beat you down.' Unfortunately, Dwight
appeared not to share her sense of humour. She said, 'When I heard
that I was supposedly really promiscuous, I said to my boyfriend,
"Honey, I'm a *traaaaaammmmmpppp*. Let's do it on the hood of the
car. Make me live up to my reputation tonight." He didn't think it
was very funny – but I do!'

Since high school, she had remained old-fashioned enough to
want a lasting relationship. And it seemed to all who knew her and
Dwight that they were a good match; perfectly happy, with never a
cross word between them. As TV chat-show host Skip E. Lowe
said, 'The joke around town was that you couldn't find either one
of them – they were always in bed.'

'The Flash' was to change all that, however. The first real shock
for Sharon was when she saw the scene after it had been edited, and
realized that much more of her could be seen than she had been led
to believe. She was not happy, 'I did that scene believing it was
going to be shot in a certain way. I was supposed to be shaded very
dark.'

That first screening of the scene was in a preview room full of
other people. As she watched it for the first time, she was horrified.
She knew that in the context of the scene, the actual 'Flash' was
right and proper, but as she said, 'It's okay that he used the shots –
but I don't think it's okay that he didn't call me into the editing
room and say, "Gee, we see more of you in this than we thought we
were going to." '

This unexpected exposure, and in front of others, left her feeling
angry and embarrassed: 'The room was full of strangers, and I felt
silly complaining. I never felt exploited by the director when I was
actually making the film. But I definitely felt exploited when I
watched it.' At the first opportunity she made her feelings known
to Verhoeven, leaving in him no doubt as to how she felt about it.
'Paul and I had a big fight over it and I wanted him to take the
scene out,' she said, 'but he wouldn't!'

After the initial shock, and knowing that the scene was there to
stay, she put it all down to experience, though not a happy one. 'I
now realize that agreeing to film it in the first place was a very

stupid thing to do on my part. I made a tremendous error of judge-
ment. I have to agree that it is right for the film. But it isn't right
for me.'

Neither was it right for Dwight. He saw the movie and his reaction to the film, and 'the Flash' in particular, led to the first – and
last – rift in the relationship. He later explained, 'I'm crazy about
Sharon. But I blushed like a fool when she showed it all. And there
was hooting and hollering from the audience.'

Sharon understood how he felt; but it seems he didn't want her
to do any more sexy scenes: 'I told her she had been suckered into
a degrading scene and that she's gotta cool it. If she gets any sexier
she's going to burn out. It's not the sort of stuff I'd want my folks
to see.'

He was, in essence, laying down ground rules to a strong-willed,
self-made woman who had purposely removed her clothing, first in
Playboy and then in *Basic Instinct*, as a way of getting to the top. It
was the end of their three-month romance, although she understood his feelings. And she did not want to be just a sex star. She
said, 'I'd have liked to be like Meryl Streep or Glenn Close and be
accepted on the integrity of my work, to have been able to do a performance like *Basic Instinct* without taking my clothes off. But
Hollywood wouldn't let me do that, so I had to make a decision.
Was I willing to strip to save my career? Ultimately, I decided I
was.'

The highly explicit sex scenes were also a problem for Michael
Douglas who decided to ask his wife, Diandra, not to see the movie.
He said, 'My wife has had to put up with a lot of questions about
her husband making love to other women on the screen, and I just
thought it would be better if she did not see the film at all, because
then she wouldn't have to comment. It was a mutual decision really.
We just thought it was best. She may see the picture when all the
fuss has died down. But not for a long time.'

He also banned his 14-year-old son, Cameron, from seeing it. 'I
was worried because it's not easy for a son to come to terms with
seeing his father making love to another woman as explicitly as we
did. We weren't actually doing it, of course, but it looked that way.
And naturally a son wants to protect his mother.' Cameron,

Before she transformed herself into a teenage beauty, Sharon thought of herself as 'a nerdy ugly duckling'. That all changed thanks to magazine articles on make-overs. 'I just looked at them and thought, "I can do that".

As a result of her own make-over, Sharon went on to become 'Miss Crawford County of 1975' and went on to enjoy a successful three-year career as an international model.

Sharon accepted a role in *Police Academy 4* (1987) 'because I needed a job'. Nevertheless, she found that the cast of stand-up comedians were 'politically astute, fun, intellectual', and she added that the film changed her 'for the good – really for the good'. (*Warner Bros, courtesy Kobal*)

The role of Arnold Schwarzenegger's wife in *Total Recal* (1989) gave Sharon her best part to date. She said that she had to 'prove my chops to earn Arnold's respect. It was tough, and I did it – that's why I liked this part'. (*Carolco/TriStar, courtesy Kobal*)

Scissors (1991) was a horror film in which she found herself stalked by a crazed killer while trapped alone in her apartment. She saw the funny side of the film and predicted 'It'll be the next *Rocky Horror Picture Show*'. (*Vidmark, courtesy Kobal*)

The notorious 'flash' scene in *Basic Instinct*; after Sharon saw it on the screen she said, 'I realize that agreeing to film it in the first place was a very stupid thing to do on my part. It is right for the film, but it isn't right for me.' (*Aquarius*)

Sliver (1993), Sharon's first film after *Basic Instinct*, was filmed under stormy circumstances which included an on-set feud with William Baldwin. She bluntly admitted, 'I didn't like Bill and Bill didn't like me. He would rather I'd been hit by a train.' (*Paramount, courtesy Kobal*)

Not a big hit but one of Sharon's favourites was *Intersection* (1994) as the wife cheated on by husband Richard Gere. She said, 'I had to beg for the part because they thought I was too vampish. I was told, "You can't play the wife because no one will believe you." I had to point out that my husband left me.' (*Kobal*)

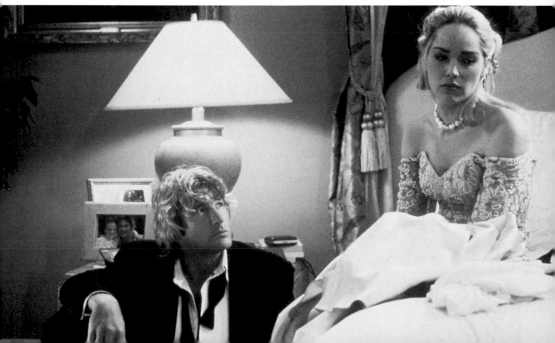

Sharon changed her image radically as a female gunslinger in the western *The Quick and the Dead* (1995). She was also the film's producer and had to fend off studio pressure to maintain her sex symbol image. 'Some people wanted me to wear a dress to ride into town. I thought, Oh yes, a gunslinger's going to ride into town riding side saddle.' (*TriStar, courtesy Kobal*)

Sharon co-starred with Sylvester Stallone in *The Specialist* (1994), and those who were expecting a clash of egos were disappointed. Sly said, 'For this kind of film, Sharon is *it* – the actress I would most want to act with.' (*Warner Bros, courtesy Kobal*)

For her performance as Ginger in *Casino* Sharon received the best reviews of her career, an Oscar nomination and a Golden Globe Award.

(*Kobal*)

Sharon Stone enjoys two lifestyles: that of Private Person and that of Film Star. 'Audiences want a resurgence of the old-fashioned movie star. I think they want me to be larger than life,' she says. (*Aquarius*)

however, managed to see the film on a pirate video, along with his school-friends. Said Michael, 'You know how kids get hold of these things! Actually he thought the film was good, although he did come home from school having been asked a lot of questions and being teased by his school-friends.'

The fact was, Diandra had been unhappy about Michael doing the film at all. She said, 'Certainly there's the issue of nudity, the sexual scenes. But there were things about the script that I found offensive as a woman. Sex was presented as a form of manipulation, and violent sex was portrayed as acceptable behaviour.' But Michael Douglas insisted that a reported rift betwen them during filming didn't occur. 'None of that was true at all,' he said. 'I have a very understanding wife.' The fact that their marriage managed to survive through the off-screen extra-marital sexual adventures he ended up admitting to demonstrated how amazingly understanding she was.

Now that Sharon was the star of a film, there was literally an old scar of hers to deal with; the scar on her neck. She had spent much of her life covering it with make-up but had stopped being so self-conscious about it years before. She said, 'Liz Taylor has a scar, I have a scar – tough shit – referring to the tracheotomy scar which Taylor acquired when she nearly died during the early stages of filming *Cleopatra*. Now that she herself was headline news, Sharon was having some fun about her scar since people were wanting to know how she had got it. Teasingly, she said, 'I'm using it to create a mystery and allure about myself. I've told a lot of great stories about it already.' One tall tale she told was that she got it from a gangster, inspired by the story of how 'Lucky' Luciano had his face cut by rival gangsters. In one interview she said she acquired it during a fight in a back alley. While the scar was not such a problem for her any more, it was for the studio – which used an expensive computer process to remove it from her close-ups.

The film was finally given a 17 rating by the American censor, the Motion Picture Association of America – MPAA. In many ways the American system allowed for hard-core pornography to be shown legally, with an NC-17 rating. But such a rating for a film aimed at making a fortune was certain death, and so – as he had anticipated – Verhoeven had to trim the film (by 42 seconds) to get its 17 rating, while in Britain and throughout the rest of Europe the film was shown uncut.

When *Basic Instinct* opened in America in March 1992, gay activist groups continued their protests outside cinemas where it played. Even the National Organization For Women announced their objection to the film, calling it 'one of the most blatantly misogynistic films in recent memory'. Despite all the controversy, or perhaps because of it, it took $15 million in its first weekend.

The media frenzy over Sharon continued. Many reporters were surprised that she had a brain, and she wasn't afraid to voice her opinions. She said, 'If I were a petite, brunette, ethnic laywer, then my behaviour would be totally acceptable. But we Barbie dolls are not supposed to behave the way I do.'

That year of 1992, on 20 April, riots broke out in Los Angeles when the policemen accused of beating Rodney King were found not guilty. The disturbances spread like wildfire through South Central LA; by the end of the day, 58 people were dead and an estimated $700m million worth of damage had been done. The next day the rioting started to move away from South Central towards the major studios which, hearing that trouble was on its way, closed down. There were drive-by shootings at the gates of Twentieth Century-Fox. Then word reached the Beverly Hills community that rioters were heading that way to set the film community alight. In the event, no such thing happened, but many film folk feared for their lives throughout Los Angeles.

Sharon Stone, in her San Fernando Valley home, was prepared for them. She later said, 'My father was a great hunter and I was brought up to use a gun. I have two shotguns at home, and when the riots happened I had them both loaded.' There was the definite impression that had a single rioter come near her home, she would have fired first and asked questions later.

She had something of a passion for guns, and said that she got a great deal of joy firing off several rounds with an Uzi. 'Oh, it's wonderful!' she said. 'You put it under your arm and hold it close to your body and feel the heat of the bullets as the gun vibrates.' Of course, there was more than a hint of satire in her words, although she made it clear she was not a woman to be trifled with, under any circumstances. 'I've hit a few people, yes,' she said. 'I've knocked a couple of guys across the room.'

Despite the row over 'the Flash' between Sharon and Verhoeven, they were all hugs and smiles when they, and Michael Douglas, went to Cannes in May to promote the film at the 45th Cannes Film Festival. Sharon appeared wearing a skimpy dress with a pair of sunflowers as a bodice, the sight of which managed to get one Cannes official hot under the collar. 'It's like something from the movie,' she said. 'She couldn't possibly be wearing any underwear.' Whether she was or wasn't, she wasn't giving away any secrets. The Festival needed her that year. In 1992, it was considered to be an unusually quiet and uncontroversial affair compared with previous years. But Sharon's appearance changed all that, as did the screening of the complete, uncut version of *Basic Instinct*. Verhoeven, Douglas and Stone attended a press conference where some 2,000 journalists from around the world vied to get their questions in, like, 'Sharon were you turned on by the sex?'

Answer from Sharon: 'You have to be joking. It was hard work.'

'Michael, what is your interpretation of the film?'

Answer: 'Sex and violence.'

'Does it have a moral?'

Replied Douglas: 'No. I think it entertains you, emotionally moves you and makes you hot and scared.'

Somebody wanted to know if Sharon, having learned the martial arts for *Total Recall*, could take care of herself. She answered, 'Some guy grabbed me in the crutch at a New Year's party, so I decked him with one punch.'

Verhoeven observed, 'You would have to be a strong guy to marry her. Otherwise she'll blow you away!'

Overwhelmed by the response to her at Cannes that year, this taught Sharon what it was to be a film star. She said:

I had been there before with *Total Recall*, so I thought it might be dizzy. But it was overwhelming. I had said, 'I need two bodyguards.' But in fact I needed ten. I couldn't leave my hotel room without many people flanking me, pushing back hundreds of people clawing at me, grabbing me, chanting my name. It was that way wherever I went. It was very, very scary because Sharon Stone wasn't me any more. It was *her*. And they wanted her. I thought, 'If they're going to have her, who am I gonna have?' I really had to sit down after that and separate Sharon Stone from me, because she couldn't be me any more. Or I would go under. So, they wanted her to be big, they wanted her to be fabulous, to say this and do that. Okay, she has to be that, I made plans based on it.

Basic Instinct didn't win any awards at Cannes, but the world knew about it, and it went on to become a smash hit. In America it became the fifth most successful film of 1992 with a domestic gross of $117.6 million. In the UK it was the top film of the year with $15.5 million. Its total worldwide figure came to $265 million – and that was before it went out on video.

And all that was achieved despite the bad reviews. Some, like *Film Review*'s David Aldridge, were able to sift through the garbage to find what made the film tick. He wrote:

> There's something not quite right with it. It's not the direction which, though over-fond of the fake climax, is fairly deft. Nor is it Michael Douglas, who's fatally attractive enough for us to forgive and try to forget *Shining Through*. And it *certainly* isn't Sharon Stone who, in Hollywood's raunchiest role, is a real thigh-full. No. What's wrong is the much vaunted, three-million-dollar screenplay ... After a wham-bam start, and a gripping first 90 minutes, a resolution of increasing 'cuteness' and preposterousness comes as something of a disappointment.

Barry McIlheney of *Empire* came even closer to figuring out exactly what *Basic Instinct* was really all about:

> Certainly, Paul Verhoeven's *Basic Instinct* is an outrageous film, a great big rubbishy sort of popcorn Saturday night movie that

used to be all the rage, the kind of hugely entertaining make-believe fun to which Aunt Ethel was most certainly not invited. The kind of film, then, with bags of sex and violence, blokes being blokes, and ice-cool blondes being just that, and even a couple of quite stupendous car chases thrown in just for old times' sake. Well, *Basic Instinct* has all of these ingredients, spliced together by Verhoeven into a heady, potent mix, quite dizzying in its speed, and excellently served by some oddly convincing performances, most notable – and unexpectedly – from former *Playboy* centrefold Sharon Stone, and a refreshingly enervated Michael Douglas.

McIlheney also examined the film for allegations of homophobia and bias against bisexuals which, he wrote, 'frankly fail to hold water on closer inspection', and found it, in comparison to some Hollywood films, 'refreshingly liberated stuff', especially in regard to the relationship between Stone and Sarelli which is 'driven by something other than pure sex which seems to fuel everything else in this highly charged piece of work'.

Time Out's Steve Grant was perhaps the most enthusiastic of critics, writing, 'Viewed from one angle, Verhoeven's troubled film is a gutsy, tough West Coast cop thriller with lashings of sex and obsession ... Aided and abetted by Verhoeven's raunchy, no-holds-barred direction, Stone smoulders and snarls. If you like things unrestrained, hard, adult and off-the-rails, then Douglas and Stone are superb.'

The video release later in the year allowed a reassessment, and this time it was Phillipa Bloom writing for *Empire*:

Given a second chance in unforgiving small screen close-up, it becomes ever harder to grasp what all the hype regarding this hopelessly manipulative piece of Saturday night fluff was all about ... The problem with *Basic Instinct* seems not to be what it says about men, women and, if you must, bisexuals (which, in reality, isn't much at all), but what it *doesn't* say about human nature. Verhoeven skirts round the issue of death and desire so effectively that it's hard to tell exactly what Douglas and Stone *do* get off on, leading to the two main protagonists being cartoonish, ludicrous and entirely unrealistic. *Some* idea of motivation would certainly have helped out here; what's missing is an intellectual link in the sex and death equation. By extracting the former from the latter for the sake of mass consumption, Verhoeven has corrupted a sophisticated tale of human sexuality and eroticism and turned it into a glossy porn flick where even the sex – let alone the story – entirely fails to convince.

Verhoeven defended his film, saying, 'I feel I really succeeded in making a Hitchcock for the nineties, more sexual, a bit more evil, more provocative probably than Hitchcock would ever do, but he was limited by the period he was living in when everything was a little more puritan, and I thought he would have loved this movie.'

In comparing himself with Hitchcock, Verhoeven put himself on a pedestal which many would have argued he had no right to do. In fact, a general perception of *Basic Instinct* has been that without the charismatic and magnetic performance of Sharon Stone, the film might have otherwise turned out to be little more than a voyeuristic piece of trash to compare with Verhoeven's later masterpiece of *pure* trash *Showgirls*.

As for Sharon, she defended the film against the critical backlash with, 'This isn't a movie that's meant to make everyone feel great. It's a movie that's meant to make you feel great and wonderful and disturbed and awful and happy and angry and "I'm not gonna go and see that movie" and then you're the first one at the theatre because you want to see what it's all about. It's that kind of movie. It's sensationalistic.'

With so much money pouring in and Sharon burning red-hot, Carolco quickly decided that a sequel was called for. They began talking to Eszterhas and Stone. She demanded, and was promised, $7 million if she did it. Eszterhas apparently wanted 'more money than God'. Michael Douglas wanted nothing to do with it, but there was talk that he would appear at the begining so they could kill off his character. As for Paul Verhoeven, he was busy elsewhere, presumably preparing to make *Showgirls* and could not commit to *Basic Instinct 2*.

At least Sharon made sure that if the sequel did go ahead, she'd have a lot more control over it than on the original, and she was reported to have got together with Joe Eszterhas to work on a story-line. A Stone spokesperson said, 'She has a lot of ideas and has been involved every step of the way.' Sharon joked about who might get chosen to play her leading man. 'Let's hope he's a virile young man. That's no disrespect to Mike, but he is getting on a bit, and I think he found it tough going towards the end.' But at the back of her mind she hoped it would never happen, and as her career progressed through later films which were designed to cast off her sexy image, *Basic Instinct 2* became increasingly less likely to happen. Officially, though, she remained committed to doing it for several years.

Critics, journalists and psychologists tried to analyse the tremendous success. Sharon put it all into perspective. '*Basic Instinct* was not a documentary. It was a romp, a kind of stupid-two-box-of-popcorn movie, not as important as people want to make it out to be. It was just a good time and let's not read in a deep psychological impact. I mean, *please!* It got you gassed up, made you want to go home and make love to the person you were with. It gave you thrills and chills and made you laugh, and it was fine.'

Sharon Stone had truly arrived. In fact, she was suddenly the top female star in America, and possibly the world. Suddenly every studio, every producer, anyone making a movie wanted Sharon Stone. She was now first on every list; there was no more auditions, no more competition. She could virtually name her own price, and choose her next project. She chose *Sliver*, to be produced by Robert Evans. Her fee was $2.5 million plus ten per cent of the gross. It was a tale of murder and voyeurism, and as she read the script, by none other than Joe Eszterhas, she knew this one was going to be another sex epic. It looked set to be another box-office smash.

7

The Hollywood Sex Romp Merry-Go-Round

The part Sharon was going to play was Carly Norris, a newly divorced literary editor who rents an apartment in a Manhattan high rise – or 'Sliver' building – and anxiously tries to forget her marriage. Her new apartment offers a life high above the noisy streets, air-conditioned, calm, and complete with a telescope. She learns that the previous occupant, an attractive woman, had fallen to her death – although the audience knows she was actually pushed, but by whom is not known.

She passes her time trying to adjust to single life once more, mostly working, going to parties, and just being on her own, and finds she is haunted by the thought of the previous tenant. She also finds herself becoming entertained by looking through her telescope to spy into people's private lives in an adjacent block.

Two male neighbours take an interest in her. One is Jack Landsford, a rich novelist; the other Zeke Hawkins, the younger of the two men. Carly doesn't know it, but Zeke owns the 'Sliver' building. Neither does she know that he is an ardent voyeur, with hidden cameras placed in every room. She discovers that a number of murders have been committed in the building, and it becomes increasingly obvious that one of her two admirers is responsible. The plot takes a few twists as it tries to convince the audience that Jack is the murderer; it ultimately takes Carly far longer than the audience to realize that Zeke is in fact the culprit as she embarks on a steamy affair with him. When she finds out that he is an obsessive voyeur, with a room full of monitors allowing him to see everything going on in the building, she gets pulled into his world before discovering that he is the murderer.

It was an adaptation of the novel by Ira Levin, which producer Robert Evans had read in 1989 and had been trying since then to get filmed. His problem was that he had fallen from grace – from a great height. Back in the 1960s and 1970s, he had been one of Paramount's top producers, with hits like *The Odd Couple*, *Rosemary's Baby*, *Love Story*, *Chinatown* and *The Godfather*. He had a reputation as a hard-nosed producer with a ruthless streak. In show business virtually from birth, he was a child actor in more than three hundred radio plays and appeared as a teenager in the 1944 film *Hey Rookie*. He continued to appear in films, playing supporting roles in major films and lead roles in B-pictures, and turned his hand to producing – first at Twentieth Century-Fox, and then at Paramount where he had his biggest successes.

In 1984, he made the disastrous Francis Ford Coppola gangster musical drama *The Cotton Club*. That film's production had been fraught with problems, not the least of which was the murder of one of the film's producers. Its commercial failure was a blow to both Paramount and Evans; he was suddenly unemployable.

But what really sealed Evans' fate was when his girlfriend was arrested for *The Cotton Club* murder. He had previously been convicted of cocaine possession in 1980, for which Hollywood was prepared to forgive him, but when his name was linked with murder he had to be dropped like a brick. 'Four years ago,' Evans said in 1993, 'I was so cold that I wasn't even allowed to eat in the Paramount commissary.' Then he got a call from an agent who told him, 'If you want to get back in the business, you have to read *Sliver* by Ira Levin.'

However, Evans knew that it would take more than just a book to get him back. 'I couldn't make a deal if I had Dustin Hoffman, Al Pacino, Jack Nicholson, Warren Beatty, a script by William Goldman and William Shakespeare and everyone willing to work for nothing,' he said.

He read the book and wanted to do it. He felt it would be a monumental hit, and his drive to acquire the rights to make it became an obsession. The problem was that it had been sought by every major studio in Hollywood – with offers as high as $1.5 million – but Levin refused to sell the rights unless Roman Polanski directed it: his reason being that he believed Polanski's *Rosemary's Baby*, produced by Evans, was the only instance where a film adaptation was better than the novel. The difficulty with that was that Polanski had fled America after being charged with statutory rape, and his return would mean imprisonment.

When Warren Beatty heard about Evans' dilemma, he told the producer, 'Why don't you send him Roman's book [*Roman by Polanski*] because in the book Roman talks about how much you had to do with the making of *Rosemary's Baby*.'

Polanski had written how he was able to finish the film when Evans stepped in to prevent Paramount from taking him off the picture. So, taking Beatty's good advice, Evans sent Levin the book, making sure he highlighted the vital sections. Levin got back to him, saying, 'You can have the book for any price you want.' He got it for somewhere between a quarter of a million and half a million dollars.

Evans asked Joe Eszterhas to write the screenplay; apparently Eszterhas was in such awe of Evans that he agreed to write the first draft and discuss money later – his final fee was said to be at least as much as the amount he got for *Basic Instinct*. Next, Evans needed his star, and since the main part was a woman, he needed the biggest female star in Hollywood. At that time there was only one name to consider – Sharon Stone. It was thought her name alone would guarantee $75 million worldwide. But Sharon was in no hurry to make a decision that could affect the rest of her career; in fact, she was really busy turning down offers from people like Michael Caine who was producing *Blue Ice* and hoped she would star opposite him in the film. He said, 'Sharon Stone was our original choice, but because she wanted to maximize the high-profile publicity surrounding *Basic Instinct* she regretfully turned us down.' She regretfully turned down a lot of hungry film-makers, including Robert Evans when he came to her with *Sliver*.

Eszterhas tried to change he mind. He failed, so Evans went to her drama coach and tried to get her to persuade Sharon; she told Sharon *not* to do it! Evans got really desperate. Long after the film had wrapped, been cut and put into release, he revealed to *Empire*'s Jenny Coney:

> I told her that Demi Moore was desperate to do it and that Bruce Willis was willing to do the male lead for nothing just so Demi would get it. It still didn't interest her. We had two days left before we had to recast or lose the picture, and I tried my last shot at her. I said, 'Geena Davis is in make-up, starting Monday.' *That* got her. Suddenly she got anxious to do the picture. Of course, Geena never even read it. I never sent it to her. Demi Moore was made up too.

In Evans' opinion, it was the fact that Geena Davis had been offered *Basic Instinct* before Sharon got it, 'so she didn't want Geena to have it.'

Sharon didn't recall being *quite* that desperate when she accepted the role. She had been offered *So I Married an Axe Murderer*, opposite Mike Meyers of *Wayne's World* fame. But she wanted to play both the wife and her sister, 'but TriStar didn't want that, so it didn't feel worth doing'. It was said that she chose instead to do *The Lady Takes An Ace* for *Cheers* by brother and sister screenwriting team Glen and Les Charles, but that came to nothing.

She was offered the female lead opposite Clint Eastwood in *In the Line of Fire*. One story had it that she turned it down because Eastwood was not a major box-office star any more – a fact not borne out by the success of *Unforgiven* – but she maintained that she rejected it because 'there was nothing to her part. I told them it would be cool if they wanted to change the villain to a villainess, but the truth is, the script, as it existed, was perfect.' After she turned it down, the role went to Rene Russo, which did great things for her. In retrospect, Sharon should have accepted it; the film was a great success, particularly on the home market, and while the role was secondary to Eastwood's, it would have lifted her immediately off the sex-romp merry-go-round. (It would also have stopped her doing *Sliver*, which caused severe damage to her career from which she was very fortunate to recover.)

Sharon apparently did agree to do *Wolf* opposite Jack Nicholson, having liked the original script. But a year later, when she read it again, it had changed. 'I never felt like "the project" came along after *Basic Instinct*. Still, I just decided to go back to work. It finally came down to, "Look, you're gonna do many projects and some of them will be good and some of them won't." '

It was only after she had finished on the film that she learned of Robert Evans' duplicity in getting her to accept the role. She said, 'It is all typical of Hollywood and it's nothing new. Don't expect an easy ride in this town. But you know the only real difference for me? I struggled for years with the same problems and the same system for not much money. Now I'm paid millions to deal with it all.'

Under the managership of Sherry Lansing, Paramount welcomed Robert Evans back into the fold, and Lansing gave him every support, determined that *Sliver* would be as much her baby as anyone's. Phillip Noyce, who helmed *Patriot Games* and *Dead Calm*, was slated to direct. Sharon's leading man was William Baldwin, who had made an impact in secondary roles in *Internal Affairs* and *Backdraft*. Baldwin, aged 29, was one of four acting brothers, the most famous being Alec – who shot to stardom in *The Hunt for Red October* and later married Sharon's closest rival Kim Basinger – the others being Daniel and Stephen. Billy said, 'Occasionally I'm stopped by people who tell me I was great in *The Hunt for Red October.*'

Sliver was Billy's shot at superstardom. Production was to begin in the autumn of 1992. It was what they called in Hollywood 'a sure-fire bet'.

Publicly, Evans announced in August 1992, 'Sharon was the only one I wanted for the role. I didn't even have a second or third choice. Any girl who can cause you not to notice Michael Douglas is special.' Sharon was totally unaware that Evans had lied to her about Demi Moore and Geena Davis, and she seemed perfectly happy with her decision to do the film when she appeared at an AIDS charity event in Los Angeles in August with her new boyfriend, Chris Peters (the son of producer Jon Peters), where they kissed and canoodled.

Before filming commenced, Evans said, 'It's the first time that the taboo fantasy of voyeurism has been explored without being exploited.' What would ultimately end up on film could not have been anything other than exploitation. Evans was enthusiastic about the subject, and said, 'It's *everyone's* fantasy.' If he made the film under that assumption, it may go some way to explaining why it was not the success he expected. But there were other reasons too.

Filming did not get off to a good start. In November a second unit camera team was sent to Hawaii to film vital location shots for the final scene. Their helicopter crash-landed on the slopes of the Kilauea volcano, which cameraman Michael Benson and his associate Chris Duddy were filming. The pilot managed to radio for help and, having spent the night on the slopes soaked with rain, they survived and were rescued with their precious footage intact.

Back in America, shooting on the first unit under Noyce's direction also got off to a rocky start. Sharon had approved the casting of Baldwin but, in preparation for their work together, she went out with him in the hope of striking up a warm relationship. Something went drastically wrong that evening; she reported back to Evans, 'I went out on a date with him and didn't want to kiss him good night.'

Baldwin told Evans, 'I didn't even try.' It was obvious that theirs was not going to be a warm working relationship.

Filming got under way in New York in October. Much of the action took place in the Manhattan apartment block, and for these scenes Evans rented a duplex penthouse in the seven-year-old Morgan Court on Madison Avenue. It had stunning views of the Empire State Building, the Chrysler Building and East River, and came complete with two bedroom/bathroom suites, a whirlpool bath, a huge 19 foot kitchen and a wraparound balcony. All the rooms were double height. Shortly after filming was completed there, the apartment went on sale through Sotherby's International Realty; its London office in Bond Street had it priced at £700,000.

Before long there were problems on the set. Sharon, probably feeling that she was about to have her body exploited in the same way as it was on *Basic Instinct*, joined forces with Billy Baldwin to complain that some of the sex scenes were unnecessarily explicit. Evans told them that the film wouldn't work without the scenes. To his displeasure, Noyce agreed with the actors. So Evans laid down the law.

He later stated some kind of admiration for Sharon, saying, 'She's got balls like Mike Tyson,' but when he came to write his autobiography, *The Kid Stays in the Picture*, he said, 'I would rather clean toilet bowls than make another movie with her.' He wrote that he came to regret persuading her to make the film. It is fair to add here that Evans also lambasted Jane Fonda as 'a pain in the ass', Barbra Streisand as 'a piece of stone', and said that Dustin Hoffman 'did not stand by me in the bad times'. Evans also wrote about Ryan O'Neal and Robin Williams, among others, in a less than fair light. Robert Evans, plagued by troubles brought on by his own dark obsessions, his failed marriage to Ali McGraw and downfall as a highly successful producer, had become an embittered man.

Sharon loved working with Tom Berenger who played Jack, the novelist next door. He began his film career hesitantly in the Paul Newman role in *Butch and Sundance: The Early Years*, and for years tried to live down the image of being a young Newman. He never quite achieved superstardom, but he has given good solid performances in leading roles in films like *Shattered* and *Gettysburg*. Of him, Sharon said, 'He is a complete gas, a seasoned professional. Once during rehearsal when I was moaning, "Tom, I don't know what to do," he said "You're a soldier of the cinema – march on!" He's a good, old-fashioned guy, happily married, kids. Regular, you know. I like regular.'

Sharon later said, 'I have no problem with the sex scenes. I read the script and thought it would make a good movie, irrespective of the sex scenes.' Evans thought she read the script and saw it as *Basic Instinct 2*, and that's what frightened her off initially. It would probably be true to say that she would have preferred *not* to have gone straight into another erotic thriller. On the other hand, she recognized that if the world now suddenly found her sexy after being told for years that she wasn't sexy enough, she would not try to persuade them otherwise. Her sex symbol image was something she saw as a tool, and she refused to take it seriously.

Said Sherry Lansing:

She has a great sense of humour about her sex image. I saw her just after *Basic Instinct* was released, before her celebrity became so enormous, and I was very impressed. She's not afraid to be who she is. I just adore her. Not even speaking professionally – speaking as a person meeting another human being – I just liked her. There is a directness to her that I find thoroughly refreshing. I can't say that we became friends because it's not like we have lunch every week, but I had a real special empathy with her.

I think what people respond to on-screen, other than the fact that she's a wonderful actress, is this kind of *person*. You feel a presence in the room when you're talking to her and I think that comes across on screen. There's not an incredible bullshit trait to her.

Sharon had yet another controversial scene, masturbating in the bath, unaware that the whole building is wired with hidden cameras. The scene as written, in which Carly is stimulated from looking at a photograph of a naked man, did not strike Sharon as being particularly realistic. 'I laughed when I read it,' she said, 'because it was so unlikely and so male-based. Women are very rarely motivated by a photograph. I told Phillip Noyce, "Look women just don't do that." Fortunately he listened.' She said he was 'mind-bogglingly supportive, and provided a space where I could try stuff, let this kind of honest female behaviour be filmed. It didn't become an exhibitionistic sort of male fantasy of what a moment like that means to a woman. I suppose something so sexually direct, yet so non-exhibitionistic is going to unsettle people. But you know how it is with sexuality.'

She even conducted something of a questionnaire among the

female members of the cast and crew. 'I wanted their input and the guys were overruled.'

She felt that when it came to be filmed it had to show 'how some women feel privately about sex. The result was that it became very sexually direct. It was not exhibitionist – with back arching and me writhing around or flicking my tongue around my mouth – but it probably looked so intense and so real that I suppose it might have been unsettling for some people. After I filmed the scene, my friend Mimi Craven and a few other women watched the playbacks and gave their approval. They felt it looked real and something that we could identify with.'

Going into the film, Sharon had hoped that the sexual content in *Sliver* would prove more honest than it was in *Basic Instinct*. '*Basic Instinct* was about fantasy,' she said. 'I mean, who makes love like that? All back-bends and an orgasm every second! And who has such confidence to rip off all their clothes?' Describing Carly as 'fragile, damaged, vulnerable, insecure about sex', she continued, 'This time, my character is more real, and women will recognize all her insecurities. She has spent most of her life with one man and she is frightened about starting a new relationship. She is shy and scared about making love with someone else. I have tried to do it in a way women go about their private lives – me included. But, you know, I have no more answers than anyone else about the perfect way to start a relationship or make love for the first time with someone new.'

It was said there was a shot of Baldwin full-frontal. His contract stipulated that he would only appear nude from the back, so if the shot did exist, it was excluded from the final cut. Baldwin later maintained that there never was a full-frontal shot.

Typically, rumours circulated that Sharon and Baldwin were lovers. Nothing could have been further from the truth, but it may have helped the publicity machine to make people believe that the two stars who were engaging in some of the most sizzling sex scenes ever filmed were just as hot off the set.

The truth was that Sharon and Billy had not grown any fonder of each other since the first exploratory date. If anything, they were becoming increasingly hostile. One day Sharon lost her temper while waiting for Baldwin to turn up on the set. She stormed to his trailer where he was on the phone to his girlfriend, Chynna Phillips, pounded on his door and yelled, 'Get your ass out here.' He spent twenty more minutes on the phone. Later that day he fluffed his lines. Sharon told the crew, 'See? This is what I have to work with!'

If anyone thought she was the one being awkward, they might have needed reminding that it was on her shoulders more than on anyone else's that the weight of the picture was being carried. That's what it meant to be a *star*. Baldwin was not really a star, but to some it seemed he was behaving like one, though not in the professional sense.

He failed to redeem himself during filming in a restaurant scene in which Sharon had to remove her panties as part of the couple's daring sexcapades. In front of the entire crew, he joked, 'Me and the rest of the world have already seen it and it's no big deal!' On another occasion, after finishing a love scene, he was reported to have told a crew member, 'Thin lips, okay breath!'

Later, when the feud hit the headlines, Baldwin called Sharon 'a paean to lipstick lesbians' in an unrestrained interview. Sharon told Stephen Rebello for *Empire*, 'Well, *he* may be a lesbian! I mean, Billy's 29 and seems so *young*. I come from Pennsylvania where guys are just sort of regular. No bullshit. They're the guy, you're the girl. In Hollywood, it seems to me, the lines are a lot fuzzier. I like most people I've worked with in the business. My votes out on Billy. I never really quite got his trip. He plays a character that was very weird, but I never got up to speed on his deal, like whether he was, "I'm in character" or "I'm out of character". Know what I mean?'

A couple of years later, Sharon was able to reflect on what an excruciating experience it had been making *Sliver*. 'I didn't like Bill and Billy didn't like me and I don't think that's a big secret. He would rather I'd been hit by a train. That was a difficult production. It was a bad mix from head to toe. I actually gained weight on that movie because I was having such a miserable experience.'

Almost every evening when she left the studio, she stopped off at her favourite restaurant in Hollywood, Rosco's Chicken and

Waffles, where they served fried chicken, scrambled eggs, waffles and corn bread, all of it 'real *greasy*'. She said, 'I'd call on the car phone when I was leaving the studio and order for about six people, but really it was all for me. I ate and ate and ate.'

Despite her fame, Sharon never exploited her own family fortunes and misfortunes, and actually asked all her old friends and neighbours back in Meadville to refrain from speaking to the Press about her or her family. Of course, many of them were too overwhelmed by their old friend being just about the most famous person in the world and some of them did spill the beans. But nobody ever came up with a derogatory story or comment about her.

What she had kept particularly quiet was her work as a volunteer with abused girls. Not even sister Kelly knew; making a success of her own life while Sharon was making her bid for superstardom, she had long given up nursing and taken to running a marketing company. 'I was earning tons of money and had a Jag,' she said, 'and I had different dates every day and was in great shape.' Kelly rented a luxury apartment in a condominium, and was truly – as her father had always taught her to do – standing on her own two feet.

All that changed when she fell down a staircase in a shopping centre, smashed her kneecap and ripped ligaments in her leg. A subsequent operation resulted in complications, and she was left wheelchair-bound and in constant pain. Unable to work, she began to use up her savings. She recalled, 'I was thinking, "Why go on living?" I thought I was going to be handicapped for the rest of my life. I was desperate.' Her only respite was due to the fact that there was a tennis court nearby, and although she could not see the games being played, she could hear them, which served to concentrate her mind on something other than her pain. She said, 'At my worst, when I lay in my bedroom in excruciating pain, it was only the sound of people playing tennis on the court below that kept me going. Following the games kept me from spilling over the edge.'

Sharon was a frequent visitor. Said Kelly, 'She would sit on the bed, holding my hands, and we would listen to the tennis together.' Then, on Christmas Eve, Kelly's doctor told her that she needed immediate surgery to correct the problems that had arisen from the earlier operation. She would have to go into hospital shortly after Christmas; she was in pain and depressed. That evening Sharon called her on the phone, telling her, 'Get dressed. I'm taking you out.'

Kelly told her, 'I'm not going anywhere.'

Sharon was insistent. Kelly complied, and when Sharon came to get her, she figured she was going to some première, or just out to eat at some fashionable restaurant. To her surprise, they wound up at the hostel where Sharon had been secretly working. 'It was a turning point,' said Kelly. 'Sharon was cruel to be kind. I was so full of self-pity. When she took me to the centre that night, I was in no mood to be charitable because of my own self-pity.'

Charity workers told Kelly about the summer camp they ran for these abused children, and suggested she might like to help them the following summer. Sharon immediately volunteered her; Kelly was furious, but Sharon told her that she could really help these kids and, reminding her of her reasons for once wanting to be a nurse, she told Kelly she could start up her own charity.

'How am I going to do that like this?' asked Kelly.

'You'll figure it out.'

The next day, Christmas Day, the whole Stone family gathered at Sharon's house; it was a family tradition to be together at that time of year. Father Joseph carried Kelly, and as she remembered it, 'everyone was doing their best to act normal'. She even managed to walk into the kitchen, sending Sharon and their mother into floods of tears.

Kelly went into hospital for her operation, and shortly after received a call from Sharon, phoning from the set of *Sliver*. 'One of the women I'm working with has a condo for sale,' she said, 'and you'll never believe where it is.' Kelly didn't have a clue, so Sharon told her, 'It's on the first floor of your building overlooking the tennis court. It will be ready for you when you come home from hospital.'

The condo was a late Christmas present from Sharon to her sister. Kelly acknowledged, 'Ultimately she is my biggest supporter. No one will ever get me to say a bad word against her.' She was true to her word, refusing to make any comment when Sharon became the target of a media attack in which she was painted as a scarlet woman, a home-wrecker and a husband-snatcher.

Behind the troubled scenes of *Sliver*, something else was going on that had obviously been kept discreetly under wraps. Sharon had begun a relationship with the film's co-producer Bill MacDonald. They met in October at the onset of filming, but it wasn't until the film was in the can that Sharon owned up to her latest love.

The problem was, MacDonald was married. His wife of only five months was Naomi; though they had been together for ten years, during which time he had worked hard to become a success. Naomi was a successful journalist in her own right, but she stood by him in his drive to succeed. Their friends used to say that they had a courtship and a friendship that had lasted longer than most marriages.

Sliver seemed to spell success for him at last. It also spelled personal disaster.

8

The Blonde, the Producer and the Jilted Wife

Filming on *Sliver* was completed in February 1993, which was when MacDonald decided to tell Naomi that he and Sharon were in love. What actually happened in the weeks building up to this, and during subsequent weeks, is somewhere to be found in the much publicized soul-baring by a woman scorned, and the little information that Sharon has given undoubtedly in her own defence.

According to Naomi's story, it was in February 1993 that MacDonald came home and talked about how he was no longer sure of wanting to 'be the man that I have to be' because he was going to have to 'lie, cheat and compromise my integrity'. He told her she stood for everything that was 'noble and good' about himself – that she *was* him, that she was his soul – but he no longer wanted to be 'the noble and good old Bill MacDonald'. He said that in order to destroy himself, he would have to destroy her. Then he told her that Sharon Stone was in love with him. According to Naomi, he said that Sharon had been to a psychic who told her she and Bill had been lovers in a previous life.

Sharon said that she met Bill in October 1992, which is when *Sliver* began filming, although they may not have begun their relationship for some weeks. She also understood that his marriage was already in trouble. Naomi stated that Bill had told her Sharon had had nothing to do with him on *Sliver*.

As for the 'psychic' tale, Sharon later said, 'My grandmother had always said that as soon as I met the man of my life, I would recognize him at once. I have met him. His name is Bill MacDonald.'

Naomi said that Bill was pretending to believe in 'the garbage about her and Bill being past-life lovers', and she declared that the whole affair was the only thing that was 'paranormal'. She also claimed that MacDonald said Sharon was so 'overcome by the nearness' of him that she fainted in his presence. But he assured her that he and Sharon had not slept together because he did not want to shame Naomi. She later said that she heard that Sharon had actually told MacDonald, 'You cannot touch me until she or you are out of the house.'

Naomi, although devastated, said that she could understand how a man would be attracted to Sharon Stone. Determined to show him what he meant to her, and equally determined not to play the jilted wife, she made him his favourite dinner that evening; then they danced to their favourite Grateful Dead track, 'Ripple', then walked along the beach in the moonlight. She said they made love that night 'as we had never done before'. It turned out to be their last night together.

The next morning he pleaded with her for time to 'wrestle with the demons placed within him by Sharon'. She agreed to give him time and flew out that day to her home town in Ohio to be with her family. There she discovered she was five weeks' pregnant.

Some days later she flew back to Los Angeles to inform MacDonald that he was going to be a father, hoping it would put their life together back in place. Arriving home, she could tell that he had not slept there since she left for Ohio; she knew that he must be staying at Sharon's. She managed to get him on his car phone and told him to come home to hear some news.

When he arrived, she told him about the baby. She said he was horrified, and immediately called Sharon on the mobile phone to tell her his wife was pregnant. Naomi claimed that she could hear Sharon screaming, 'Where are you? Why aren't you here?' He told her that he needed to be at home because of his wife's 'emotional state'. According to Naomi, she heard Sharon say, 'Why does she have to talk to you about this? Doesn't she have any friends?'

Naomi asked MacDonald how he could love someone who seemed to heartless. Further phone calls followed – one lasting forty minutes – and when Naomi answered the phone, it would go dead.

MacDonald told Naomi that he was destroying her life, his child's life, and himself. The trauma continued, interrupted from time to time by phone calls – presumably from Sharon – and when they finally got around to discussing the baby, he told Naomi, 'You can do what you like with it.'

That seemed to indicate that the marriage was well and truly over. Naomi left him and went to stay with her brother, Jerry, who lived in Los Angeles. A few days later she miscarried. MacDonald's own family offered her support, and she went to live with his sister, Sheila, in Houston.

Sharon and Bill began to go out in public together, and were even invited to spend an evening with President Clinton; it was said that Sharon introduced Bill as her fiancé. News reached Naomi in Texas that Bill was telling everyone that Sharon had not been responsible for breaking up his marriage, a move which Naomi saw as an act of desperation to keep Sharon in a good light. According to Naomi, a close friend informed her that Bill was saying that during his last night with her, he had been afraid she would commit suicide with barbiturates, which was why he had stayed the night. She claimed he also spun a lie about her holding him at gunpoint on their penultimate night together. The only people who will ever really know the truth of what went on are Bill and Naomi themselves.

Naomi further claimed that after returning to Los Angeles, Bill came to see her and said that they had to get their stories straight – that she should say that he was never at home and she didn't like the Hollywood life, so he had left her. She told Bill that he and Sharon could say what they liked – she was going to tell the truth.

Having protected him for so many years, she was prepared to lie for him, 'but I won't lie for Sharon Stone'.

He then presented her with papers to sign, formalizing their separation, telling her to seriously think about changing her story. He hoped no one would contact her because he and Sharon intended to keep a low profile. She told him he had taken away all her hopes for their future, and given them to someone else.

According to her, he said, 'I got too close to fame. Why don't you just go away? You are so noble.'

She did. Then she went on television to brand Sharon as a home-wrecker, and talked to the world's press, claiming MacDonald's relationship with Sharon was mere sexual attraction and an attempt to grasp what Naomi described as 'the keys to power and the attainment of all he wanted'. She said, 'Bill and Sharon may feel they can live with what they've done, but they can't step on me and sweep me under the carpet.'

Throughout the time Naomi publicly displayed her heartbreak, she vented most of her anger at Sharon. 'I could say nasty things but I won't stoop to her level,' said Naomi, then added, 'She knows she took my lover, my husband, my future, my life. She knew what she was destroying.'

Whatever the real truth, what Naomi really painted was a portrait of herself as a woman who had been betrayed in the worst way. Sharon kept mainly quiet about the affair, although perhaps in reference to how she had perceived the relationship between Naomi and Bill to be, she said, 'Our love is stronger.'

Bill, in Naomi's story, came across as a man under an unhappy spell who 'pathetically' told her in a conversation they had after the split, 'I have no life now – I am a vagabond.'

It all finally quietened down when none other than Joe Eszterhas left his wife and children to take up with Naomi MacDonald. But by then a considerable amount of damage had been done to Sharon's image.

Phillip Noyce worked long and hard on cutting *Sliver*, and in the editing room it became apparent that Sharon in close-up was far more effective than in shots where she shared the frame with other actors, so he chose more close-ups of her where normally a 2-shot might have sufficed, effectively giving Baldwin less screen time than he might otherwise have had.

Meanwhile, Sharon got on with making plans and decisions. She didn't want to sit around waiting to see how *Sliver* would come out; nor did she wish to go on making the same kinds of films which, it seemed – based solely on the success of *Basic Instinct* thus far – the public preferred to see her in, and she had tried to portray herself as a movie star in the way she believed everyone wanted her to be. In this respect she had tried to maintain a low, dignified profile throughout Naomi's much-published revelations.

'In the first eighteen months after *Basic Instinct* I felt that I made a lot of choices for the public,' said Sharon, 'like where to go, how to behave. I felt that the responsibility of being famous was to exemplify positive behaviour, which I still believe. But I had stopped allowing myself room for error. And I had lost the ability to say, "Hey, I made a mistake, so sue me!" '

Fortunately, she had developed a somewhat thick skin, essential for survival in Hollywood, and in reference to the criticism aimed at her by other women for promoting what they considered to be 'the Barbie doll image', she said, 'I let it pass. I don't take myself very seriously. I like to make people laugh. It's like, if a woman can't be happy for another woman's work, they have to go to work on that.'

Her next choice of movie would not be for the benefit of the public, nor for her critics – which meant she would have to wade through the mountain of 'Barbie doll' scripts sent to her. She said, 'I was tired of playing dumb blondes who always ended up in the sack. And I was incredibly bored making *Sliver*. It was time for a change. I didn't want to play the same part over and over again.'

Even though *Sliver* had not yet had the chance to consolidate her success, she nevertheless received plenty of firm offers for films not yet written – she only had to say 'Yes' to make a fortune. Among these was the sequel to *Basic Instinct*; she was still hesitating on that one, especially after *Sliver*.

What did interest her more was an offer from Dino De

Laurentiis, who wanted her to star in *The Immortals*, based on the novelized account of the affair between Marilyn Monroe and the Kennedys, leading up to her death. The carrot to do that one was a cool $6 million. But she was more interested in *not* having to portray Monroe; she suggested they turn the characters into fictional people. They told her they'd get back to her on that, but it seemed unlikely the project would go ahead with her.

The one she finally chose to follow *Sliver* was *Intersection*, an American remake of a popular French film. Richard Gere was starring as a wealthy architect, Vincent Eastman, who is torn between his wife Sally and a ravishing sex-hungry beauty, Olivia. The only thing that holds the marriage together is their 13-year-old daughter. Finally, the time comes for Vincent to make his decision, but fate takes a hand with a tragic car crash.

Richard Gere had been experiencing a few ups and downs in his career. Once a top box-office attraction, he had peaked during the 1980s and, while continuing to work during the early 1990s, he was no longer right on top. Not that he was bothered. He obviously felt he had arrived at a point in his life when he could afford to choose projects because he liked them and not because they were designed to rake in hundreds of millions in profits. He was also fascinated with French cinema, and had taken the opportunity to remake French films twice previously, with *Breathless* and *Sommersby*, one of his biggest successes of more recent years.

When Paramount first came to Sharon with *Intersection*, it was to offer her the part of the sultry Olivia. She told them she would like to play the wife, but they were most reluctant to cast her in a role that was bereft of any real glamour while to them she seemed perfect for the sex interest. She recalled, 'I had to beg for the part because they thought I was too vampish. I was told, "You can't play the wife because no one will believe you." I had to point out that my husband left me. It took a while to talk them into testing me for Sally, but I insisted because I knew what she'd been through.'

When Sharon offered to *test* for the role, it was something Paramount could hardly refuse her. Now the kind of star who didn't have to test for anything, she had producers breaking down her door with firm offers and large amounts of money. So she tested for director Mark Rydell who had been making films for a long time – his first film, D.H. Lawrence's *The Fox*, was in 1968. He went on to make some very fine films which often produced outstanding performances, including *The Reivers*, which starred Steve McQueen and brought Rupert Crosse an Oscar nomination as Best Supporting Actor; *The Cowboys*, in which John Wayne gave one of his most outstanding and underrated performances; *Cinderella Liberty*, which brought Marsha Mason an Oscar nomination and was both a big critical and commercial success; *The Rose*, for which Bette Midler was Oscar nominated; and *On Golden Pond*, which gave both Henry Fonda and Katharine Hepburn Oscars. Rydell knew all about actors, and how to get the best out of them. He liked Sharon, and gave her the role she wanted.

Gere was impressed, not only with Sharon's test but with her courage to go against type and her determination not to take no for an answer. He said, 'This is a very different kind of role for Sharon.' She could not have been totally oblivious to the fact that she was embarking on a film role that might well have proved Joe Eszterhas right – he believed her image was set in stone. But she was not willing to sit back and make easy choices. Besides which, *Sliver* may well have seemed to some to be an easy choice to follow *Basic Instinct*, and that proved to be so.

Sharon asked for, and got, a fee of $3 million. She had no qualms about getting paid such a high figure; she said, 'I earned this. I didn't come out here to Hollywood and say I was the greatest actress in the world right out of the chute. Sometimes I was good, sometimes I was really stinky. They didn't owe me anything. I stayed. I held my place in line. They got to my number.'

She was well aware of the power she had acquired as an actress. 'They'd pay me to play Lassie,' she said. 'Believe me, when people say, "We want to pay you X million to do this movie," I won't be the girl who hangs back saying, "Oh, I really don't deserve it." I'll be, "Uh-huh, hand it right over." '

Sally, she said, was just the kind of part she was looking for. She was certainly not past it at the age of 35, but she knew that she would not continue to look as good as she did for ever. 'I'm looking forward to getting my teeth into some meaty roles,' she said. 'I feel totally in step with Father Time.'

She was aware that even at that age she was fighting to keep her body together, and said with a laugh, 'It's gravity. I don't mind using a body double in the future – who cares? Bring me a big sandwich and let someone else do the nudity.' In fact, she hoped never to have to strip in films again. 'I've had it with taking my clothes off. It's time to let someone else take the heat.'

The role of the ravishing beauty went to a relative newcomer, Lolita Davidovitch. Sharon was completely happy to be playing 'an upright, waspy, 40-year-old with hair pinned to within an inch of its life'. She said she wanted to 'grow as an artist'. Joe Eszterhas thought it a bad idea, saying that for her to try to change her screen persona 'could be a very dangerous process. Stallone was certainly hurt when he decided to become a yuppie comedian. She should keep that in mind.'

Sharon was not so naïve as to believe that she could shake off her sexy image completely, and said, 'I don't have the Olivia de Havilland sense about myself. I'm much more Scarlett O'Hara.'

She also decided to try her hand at producing. Having long wanted to be in control of her career she set up her own company and chose to do, of all things, a Western. Since Clint Eastwood's *Unforgiven* had become such a monumental hit the previous year and was nominated for several Oscars (for which it won Best Film, Best Director and Best Supporting Actor for Gene Hackman), Hollywood had become gripped by Western fever. Several Wild West projects were being planned, including Kevin Costner's epic *Wyatt Earp*, its rival *Tombstone*, and *Geronimo*.

Sharon believed that a Western was the very thing to break the sex symbol mould. The screenplay she picked was *The Quick and the Dead*, the tale of a female gunslinger who rides into the town of Redemption to participate in an organized showdown contest which, like the gladiatorial combats of old, could only be won by the survivor left standing. Losers were the dead ones! It had a very black feel to it, with the town being run by a psychotic killer called Herod. The twist in the tail was that the female gunfighter's real purpose in coming to Redemption is to kill Herod in revenge for murdering her father.

It had been written by British film director Simon Moore, who had made *Under Suspicion*, but his intention was to produce and direct the film. When Stone offered him $1 million for the script, it was impossible for him to turn her down even though he would not be producing the film himself. Nevertheless, he still hoped to direct. Unhappily for him, Sharon had other ideas; she wanted Sam Raimi, who made *Darkman* and *Army of Darkness*, to direct. 'Sam was the only person on my list,' she said. 'I don't think it's the kind of picture just anyone could have made because of the kind of material it is.'

Sharon went to Tristar with the project and they gave a tentative agreement to back it to the tune of $30 million. At that time, with *Basic Instinct* still making money, it was thought that Sharon Stone was a walking, talking gold mine.

In early March, Noyce had his final cut on *Sliver* ready for the ever-diligent Motion Picture Association of America to view. They reported back that to avoid the film getting an NC-17 rating – the certificate for legalized pornography – it needed 110 changes. Noyce called them and objected, and a furious row ensued. But the MPAA would not give way.

Evans joined in the battle, accusing the board of being disturbed by the subject matter. 'Voyeurism is everyone's hidden fantasy,' he said, 'and a lot of people just don't want to admit it. I think the rating board members were unnerved by it because it may be their hidden fantasy too.'

After all the hype on *Basic Instinct*, Sharon became bored with the whole subject of screen sex, but she was mystified by the attitude towards her films. 'Americans are much more morally judgmental,' she said. 'Sex in America – it's like everybody pretends that nobody does it. It's the weirdest thing I ever saw. Everything is motivated by sex. Every commercial, all the media, all the fitness things, selling a car – it's *all* sex!'

The film's climax had long been a point of contention between Evans and Noyce. Eszterhas's original ending featured the volcano which the second unit had risked their lives to get on film. In the story, Baldwin and Stone fly over the volcano in a helicopter, release their seat-belts and fly straight towards the lake of lava. The screen then goes blank, leaving the question of whether or not they died unanswered. Noyce favoured this ending, but Evans always hated it.

Then came the first preview, with an audience recruited from the shopping centres of LA; they were not impressed. One thought the sex scenes were 'juvenile, like some high school scholar writing on the walls in a locker room'. Most found the sight of soft-core voyeurism too much of a surprise, with comments like 'sleazy' and 'gratuitous'. But the greatest criticism was for the ending of the film, which confirmed Evans' opinion. 'I never thought it could work,' he said. 'Audiences resented, and rightfully so, the fact that, in essence, the killer got away without being caught.'

Over the next three days, Eszterhas wrote five new endings and then went into seclusion with Naomi. There had been none of the bitter wranglings over the script which he had experienced on *Basic Instinct*. With *Sliver*, he did the job he was paid to do and seemed not to care too much about what else happened, even though he was credited as an executive producer of the film. When asked which ending he thought they were using, he said, 'They could've fucked with it by now for all I care.'

On 28th March, Evans collapsed on the Paramount lot with a suspected heart attack and was rushed to hospital. Waiting for an angiogram, he continued his attack on the MPAA board, saying, 'They're scared shitless of the subject matter. I knew when I attacked this subject matter that there was going to be a lot of heat. They're all voyeurs, probably.' He later wrote that of all the actors who gave him trouble, Sharon Stone was 'the only one who gave me a heart attack'. To blame her for his health problems perhaps said more about Evans than it did about Stone.

That night in hospital he dreamed of two new endings, and the next day he phoned his secretary from his hospital bed to dictate the two new scenes.

When Evans and Noyce called the cast back at the end of March to reshoot the two new endings, the actors were not told which one would be used. The mystery did nothing to lighten the mood among the actors who were still tense and, in the case of Stone and Baldwin, bordering on hostile. There were also some additional shots, and a still photo which Noyce needed showing Berenger and Polly Walker in a kinky S&M photograph. Berenger was furious, and refused to do the shot on the grounds that it wasn't in the script and had not been detailed in the reshooting schedule. 'You can't keep doing these things,' he said. 'I'm not here as a slave. You've tricked me into things, and I'm holding you now to this contract.' He even went so far as to accuse Noyce of 'sneaking around and manipulating' the cast.

Noyce tried to explain that this was just a way of demonstrating his character's perversion. 'That sounds like *your* perversion,' Berenger told him. 'You go do that shit, but not me.' Polly Walker agreed with Berenger, and Noyce had to resort to using body doubles. The version that the board finally passed was still considered highly explicit, with scenes of sexual intercourse, masturbation and even shots of a penis as seen on video monitors within the film.

The next test screening was a success. 'They whooped and hollered,' Evans recalled.

William Baldwin seemed to speak for everyone concerned when he said, 'There is voyeurism and there is murder and there's sex and there's Sharon Stone. What else could you want?' Everyone agreed. The film had to be a box-office winner.

Sharon was asked to host the Scientific and Technical Awards at the 1993 Oscars, which seemed to consolidate her importance, and she accepted $1 million to make TV commercials for Pirelli Tyres filmed in Europe. In them she played a movie star – pretty much herself really – who lands in a private plane and notices that the tyres on the chauffeured car waiting for her are Pirelli. Her handsome chauffeur drives too sedately for her liking and she lures him into the back seat with what appears to be a promise of passion. But instead she jumps into the driver's seat and puts her foot down.

If imitation is indeed the most sincere form of flattery, then in 1993 Sharon knew she had arrived for sure. In the tradition of film spoofs established by *Airplane* and *The Naked Gun,* and thereafter continued with the likes of *Loaded Weapon, Hot Shots* and *Repossessed,* came *Fatal Instinct* starring Sharilyn Fenn, Sean Young,

Kate Nelligan and Armand Assante. The poster said it all; a woman in a red dress sits on a wooden chair, smoking a cigarette and crossing her legs. Across her knees are the words 'Opening Soon'.

The poster was enough to kick up a storm that almost rivalled the outrage from certain groups over the real *Basic Instinct* when press kits, with posters included, were sent to news rooms around America. Lady news editors tore down the posters after male colleagues had put them up. One woman complained to MGM that the posters were 'inappropriate'. A spokesman for MGM said they would send out replacements, saying, 'I'm sure they will find it equally inappropriate, but we find it equally hilarious.'

The controversy was enough to bring a smile to Sharon's face, not least because she had previously been the target for such outrage, but perhaps most of all because her first major starring role had been given the *Airplane* treatment, which in itself was an indication of the impact she and the film had made.

And to consolidate that she had truly arrived and her name was now a household word, the movie version of *The Flintstones* included a character whose name was, of course, Sharon Stone.

A year earlier, at the time of *Basic Instinct*, Sharon could do and say no wrong. The lies about her wild sex life and drug abuse were largely ignored as the world waited with baited breath to see the woman Hollywood and the media were calling the 'new Marilyn Monroe'. But the public were outraged with her over her relationship with Bill MacDonald; she was no longer the lovable sex symbol, but a home-wrecker.

For the first time she was the target of bad press. It didn't help that in March she announced that Bill MacDonald had given her an engagement ring. She also talked of wanting babies. 'I want to get married and I want to have babies. I want to have babies more than anything in the world.' Of their early days together, she said: 'It is weird living together at first because you find yourself flipping out when you leave your underwear lying around!'

The problem was that she was seen to be marrying – indeed, *stealing* – another woman's husband, and he was perceived by the public to be a treacherous two-timing swine. Sharon tried to tell the public, 'He's so square. He's square, square, square, square! I love it.' She described him as 'so old-fashioned. He is so macho with his husky voice. It's terribly exciting after all these hippie guys with long hair and sweet artistic tempers.'

She also said that when he told her to 'Come here – now!' she ran to him, 'because I know it will be good when I get there'. Her life was 'full of joy. I'm in love and I'm really, *really* happy about it.' But as lovesick as she was, she had still not abandoned one important rule in her life: 'No one is going to take control of me.' The question then was, did she want someone she could control? She said, 'The point is, finding someone over whom I don't have complete control.'

Sharon tried to play down the vision people had of her as having sex at every opportunity. 'I think sex as sex is not really very interesting to me any more,' she said. 'Sex as sensual, loving communication is very interesting to me – but not every five seconds. That would be too much to cope with. Real loving, fabulous, generous, intimate sexuality is not something you want to have every five seconds.' One newspaper pointed out that it had taken her thirty-five years to learn the true meaning of physical love – *and* it had taken another woman's husband to teach her!

The media were full of stories that took her generally wickedly funny quotes and turned them into something more seedy. When she jokingly told a reporter that she always wore a black bra, a G-string, a garter belt and black stockings when she met a director, she was reported as being ready and willing to flaunt her body.

In an effort to make the point that she and Bill were not in the habit of arguing, she said that the only time they argued was 'over the fact I don't wear any underwear'. She was, of course, making fun of her sexy image, but in print it gave a different impression.

The fact was that the screen star Sharon Stone had become an invention of the real Sharon Stone, and she had tremendous fun playing her. 'I mean, she is too funny,' she said of the other Sharon Stone. 'She's wild, and campy, and wears sexy clothes and says vulgar things, and lives fast and carries on – and it's fun. It's fun to be her, but I know that it's me being her.'

When she told a reporter that she had finished with Chris Peters, who was almost ten years younger than she was, because he was 'too young', she was depicted as a heartless man-eater. In fact she said, 'We sort of grew up together. He's such a loving, decent loving man and I really like him very much. But he's too young for me, or I'm too old for him, more's the point.' She was said to be writing a novel based on her own sordid life. In fact, she had joked with Stephen Rebello, 'It's my destiny that I'll write my own *Valley of the Dolls*-type Hollywood novel. My life is actually quite like *Valley of the Dolls* except that I have better clothes and hairdos. I don't know what I'll call my exposé about Hollywood, but I already have my opening sentence: "The sex change operation wasn't nearly as painful as I had anticipated. . . ." '

On 29th March she turned up at the main Oscars TV ceremony, accompanied by Bill MacDonald, giving the TV viewing public a chance to see the man himself. It gave fodder for further public pain for Naomi, who said, 'I can't pretend that I don't want to cry out in pain and anger every time I see Sharon's picture. It makes it tougher to get over the nightmare. Last week I tried to forget it for a while by watching the Oscars on TV. But there she was – Sharon Stone. It was awful to see Bill meekly standing behind her while she was interviewed. He looked like her pet. That's not the Bill I know. But it's his mess and I don't want any more to do with it.'

That night, on a TV talk show, Sharon announced that she and Bill were engaged, and said, 'We love each other very much and are committed to spending the rest of our lives together.'

In April Bill began to put the wheels into motion for a quickie divorce. He filed papers in Los Angeles stating that he believed Naomi was capable of supporting herself, and he expected that while he might have a fight on his hands over alimony, he anticipated he would soon be free to marry Sharon. Naomi, however, thought otherwise, and refused him his quickie divorce.

Despite the awful press Sharon had received, she said she cared only that people found her entertaining whether on screen or in print. 'I hope I please the audience and that they find real entertainment at the theatre and have fun when they read the articles and have fights with people over things I say.'

But she felt secure enough not to care what people really thought of her. 'I know this is my moment and at the same time, even from here, it doesn't matter if people continue to champion me or not.'

Nevertheless, it did matter.

In the spring of 1993, Sharon was voted as a contender for Most Popular Dramatic Actress by readers of *People* magazine in their annual People's Choice Awards, but she didn't win.

That same year *Première* magazine put her at number 54 in their '100 Most Important People in Hollywood', above Jane Fonda, Barbra Streisand and Goldie Hawn.

When the Paediatric AIDS Foundation ran an auction, she appeared as an auctioneer and managed to sell a Ferrari 348 Spider for $185,000, and made an extra $10,000 by offering to go for a drive with the new owner, cinema-chain owner Paul Goldenberg. 'I kept her to the offer and she kept her side of the bargain,' he said. 'It was great fun. We had a good time. She said the Spider is the only thing faster than she is!'

AIDS was a subject close to her heart, having lost a number of friends to the disease, including Rock Hudson. She tried to break through her usual wisecracking to deliver a serious message. When asked what advice she would give to young people, she replied, 'That there is no peer pressure. That's a figment of your imagination. Do not do anything because someone thinks you should. Be true to your heart and *absolutely* have safe sex because my friends are dead or dying of AIDS. It's not a joke. I'm adamant about it.'

In May, Sharon was shopping in a Los Angeles supermarket when it was held up by a gunman. He pointed the gun at her and threatened to blow her brains out if she screamed. She waited for a moment when he looked away, and then she suddenly rolled down the aisle, ran out and called the police. The gunman was arrested, but she didn't wait around to see the arrest. She said, 'I don't want him looking for me when he comes out of the slammer.'

She kept busy, making personal appearances. That summer she was at the opening of a new Planet Hollywood restaurant in Chicago, where she danced on stage with owners Bruce Willis,

Arnold Schwarzenegger and Sylvester Stallone. En route, her luggage was lost and she had to buy jeans and a black T-shirt for her dance spot. Bill sat and watched his fiancée strutting her very sexy stuff on stage, where it got so hot that Willis stripped down to his shorts and then, cheered on by celebrity guests like Melanie Griffith and Don Johnson, gave Sharon a big kiss in front of 3,500 cheering people.

What few people saw Sharon do that summer was take off with Kelly to a summer camp. After being introduced to the charity Sharon had been secretly working with that previous Christmas Eve, Kelly (now out of a wheelchair and walking with a limp) set up her own charity, Planet Hope, with big sister's help. The summer camp was to give training and medical care to homeless families. 'I know how easy it is almost to lose your home, your health and your job in a single moment,' said Kelly. 'Later, when we organized a training camp for our own charity, Sharon was there too, sleeping in a makeshift bed and eating horrible food from the cafeteria.'

There was still the job of being an actress to which Sharon eventually had to return. Offers had been pouring in, and by the summer of 1993 her house had piles of scripts mounting up. She was considering *Manhattan Ghost Story*, written by Ronald Bass, Oscar winner for his sceenplay of *Rain Man*. The script had originally been tailored for Julia Roberts after she turned it down, they came to Sharon, but she decided she was not about to take on any more roles written for someone else.

She said she was interested in an action picture called *Pin Cushion*. 'The script isn't completed, but it'll come about when it's ready.' She longed to do a comedy, but every effort to do so had failed so far. 'I suppose if I agreed to be funny *and* nude, they'd suddenly get it,' she said.

Filming on *Intersection* commenced in the summer of 1993. One morning, early in production, Sharon pulled up at the studio gates – wet hair, sunglasses, in a coma – and winding down her window she announced, 'Sharon Stone', to the guards.

'No, you're not,' they said.

'What the hell would I be doing here at five-thirty? Do I look like the kind of girl who gets up early for *fun*?'

'Sharon Stone was here the other day,' said a guard, 'and you look nothing like her. So back it up!'

Sharon finally managed to convince them, but to make sure it didn't happen again, she insisted she be given an electric key to let herself in.

The film provided Sharon with her most challenging assignment as an actress since *Year of the Gun*, and she thoroughly enjoyed herself. 'For me it was the experience of working with Mark and working with Richard,' she said. 'It was definitely one of the happiest experiences I've had on a film set. We all got on with each other, all got on with the work.'

According to Rydell, 'The chemistry between Richard and Sharon is like Gable and Lombard – rich and sexy.'

She said that it was a pleasure each day to drive home and not leave behind a day fraught with tension, having filmed simulated sex or having had to take her clothes off. Speaking of all the reviews that said she couldn't act, she said, 'What really pisses me off is all this stuff about not being able to act. That I was some blonde who just got lucky. I worked for all that I got.'

When the film was finished, it was shown to a preview audience who seemed to dislike the abrasive edge to the characters, and Paramount decided it needed cutting. Said Sharon, 'What happened to that picture as a result of test marketing and studio pressure is a crying shame because the cut of the picture before that happened was brilliantly moving. In trying to make everybody so darned likeable, they took all of the punch out of it.'

Rydell was unhappy with the changes too, but the studio that pays for a film will do whatever it thinks is necessary to make it more commercial. In the case of *Intersection*, it didn't work. But because the film was held back until 1994 before it was released, they had to wait to find out.

Having decided that she would not portray Marilyn Monroe, Sharon became interested in an idea about a film biography of Monroe's predecessor, Jean Harlow. Her short and often shocking life fascinated Sharon, who said, 'Harlow is an icon. She invented a new kind of Hollywood star but had an even sadder off-screen life than Marilyn Monroe. She was so strong and yet so vulnerable.'

Harlow was a product of the early studio star system, and her tragic life – ruled by a gangster stepfather, affairs with Mafia hoods and her part in the mysterious death of her husband Paul Bern, which we now know was murder – and ultimately her death were all part of that system. Yet the system made Harlow into a star and protected and nurtured her career – provided she kept to the rules. It was a life far removed from the one Sharon had, fighting to exist in a Hollywood where the studios no longer cared about anything other than how much your last movie made. Actors were all freelance, and had neither the safety-net nor the ruthless trappings the studios once offered, but there were still pitfalls for the vulnerable, as Sharon knew all too well.

'If I'd shot to stardom in my early twenties, like a lot of actresses, I'd be dead by now,' she said. 'I always thought I was smart and sassy and knew everything – and I'm sure I'd have rocketed straight down the road of excess to instant demise.'

The Harlow project, done twice before in the 1960s with Carol Lynley and Carroll Baker playing the original blonde bombshell in rival movies, came to nothing.

9

It Feels Great to be a Mogul

To the amazement of everyone at Paramount, *Sliver* was not the success they had expected. And the problem may well be that the bad press Sharon Stone had over the months preceding and during its release was enough to keep people away.

Others might argue that it was the bad reviews, that it was simply a matter of the film not being that good. Yet anyone in the business knows that films with lousy reviews have been extremely successful, and that movies do not need to be artistic masterpieces to be popular. In the case of *Sliver*, it suffered mainly in its domestic market, taking only $36 million at the American box office. Having cost $50 million, this was considered a disaster. Critics boasted that their analysis of the film – that it was just plain bad – was the reason for its failure. But it was not quite that simple. In fact, when MTV gave out their movie awards based on popularity, William Baldwin was voted Most Desirable Male based on his role in *Sliver*. This was probably the only award the film ever won, but indicated that it was not entirely ignored by the American public – and this was a vote by the female contingent. Baldwin, who may not have gelled with Sharon but neither was an outright egotistical villain, said he was surprised by the award. 'I've always been kind of lanky, kind of goofy-looking, so I don't understand the emphasis on my looks.'

123

Apparently, great emphasis had been on the fact that he showed his backside in *Sliver*, to which he responded, 'I really don't think I'm typecast as the actor who shows his butt all the time. If I had my choice of what I want chiselled on my tombstone – "Billy Baldwin, he was so sexy" or "Billy Baldwin, what a great actor" – I'd prefer it was not the former. I'd rather people admired me for my work.'

Unfortunately for Baldwin, *Sliver* did not propel him further towards greatness, and his subsequent films did little to improve the chances of his desired epitaph.

With Sharon's new film awaiting release, her last one a seeming disaster and *The Quick and the Dead* set to be her next, her career was moving fast, although in which direction it was hard to say. Most male stars were generally forgiven if they made a box-office flop in between making big successes, but the female stars were not accorded the same right. When Julia Roberts was big, she was very big, and when she flopped, she was no one. So was Michelle Pfeiffer ... so was every female superstar before and since. Now it was Sharon Stone's turn to be condemned.

It may well have affected her chances of getting the role of Catwoman in *Batman Returns*. Annette Bening was going to play the part, but had to drop out when she fell pregnant. The two main contenders were now Stone and Pfeiffer. Hollywood gossips, of course, made much of the contest and they gleamed with delight when Sharon boldly, and no doubt with humour, said that she would make a better Catwoman than Michelle – and for just half the price.

Of the two superstar actresses, Sharon was the one who made louder noises about wanting to have greater power in Hollywood, and she was never slow to voice her opinion that the town was dominated by men who didn't think a woman should waste her time thinking. Said one studio executive, 'Sharon has got to ease back on the throttle when it comes to saying what's on her mind. Michelle made all her moves behind closed doors, which is why she got it. Sharon was outplayed in the power politics of the business.'

Sliver's poor performance in America also affected the prospects for *The Quick and the Dead*. TriStar became nervous about going ahead with the film that would cost them around $30 million.

Although Sharon was good at publicly shrugging off the pressures and tensions of the sometimes insane industry she was in, behind closed doors she allowed only those closest to her to see her at her most angry and frustrated. 'I worked like a dog to get where I am today,' she said. 'If it hadn't been for Bill I think I would have gone mad.'

Sharon desperately wanted to be married; it may have just been her old-fashioned way or her eagerness to have babies before she reached her forties – whatever her own purpose, she was set on marrying Bill. She said, 'I hope that Naomi is done now after all her outbursts. When you let someone go it's bound to be upsetting, but enough is enough. I love Bill and we're engaged to be married. Being in love has made me a nicer person, and we'll marry one day. We're still trying to decide if it will be just us or a small ceremony – for about 2,000 people!'

Then rumours began that all was not roses between Sharon and Bill. As mentioned before, he had tried to get a quick divorce from Naomi earlier in the year, but the jilted Mrs MacDonald was not allowing him to have his way. After Sharon's public declarations about engagement, marriage and babies, any delay in resolving the situation was bound to give rise to public comment.

In August 1993, Sharon arrived in Britain for what was thought to be 'a secret date with a mystery aristocrat' who was described as 'a dark-haired minor Royal'. The anonymous witness to the couple's rendezvous in swanky Chelsea Harbour in London said, 'Sharon wasn't dressed like a movie star. She looked quite plain and obviously didn't want to attract attention. Her aristocratic partner was handsome, about 25 years old and very attentive towards her. The pair seemed very close. They had a quiet, intimate dinner, then slipped away together.'

It wasn't really all that strange that Sharon should 'secretly slip into Britain' since *Sliver* was about to open in Europe. She was, in fact, embarking on a world-wide promotional tour in an attempt to boost the film's flagging box office.

Paramount saw no reason to suppose the film would do any better overseas, but Sharon wasn't prepared to sit back and assume the same. She got on plane after plane to promote the film in country after country, earning the respect and admiration of Paramount boss Sherry Lansing who said, 'Even after *Sliver* did not do well domestically, she travelled tirelessly around the world to support its foreign bookings. Everyone who makes a movie should do that, but Sharon is one of the few who does. Arnold Schwarzenegger does it. Michael Douglas does it. That is what makes you an international star.'

While in Italy, she and Bill attended the Italian Television Awards in Milan. Italian fans were known to be over-enthusiastic in demonstrating their admiration; so, not taking any chances, she had a formidable escort consisting of a point car with two bodyguards inside, and a tail car with two more bodyguards. She thought she was safe. But as her small cavalcade approached their destination, the gathered crowd went wild and swarmed over her car until, as she put it, 'it was pitch black inside'. They pulled off the wing mirrors and the bumpers, and were rocking the car wildly. She and Bill began to really fear what would happen to them if the frenzied Italians got to them. To try to fend off the terror, Sharon actually began singing. Finally a small army of riot police got around the car and formed a human chain so that Sharon and Bill could escape.

In Britain, *Sliver* met with uniformly unenthusiastic reviews. Clive Hirschorn wrote in the *Sunday Express*:

Phillip Noyce's thriller promises to be a kind of hi-tech *Rear Window*, but finishes up as a state-of-the-art piece of soft porn schlock set in New York against a background of media glitz and glamour. Its central character is a jobbing editor for a publishing house whose salary allows her to live in a stunning 20th floor apartment in the heart of Manhattan. If you believe that, you will have no difficulty in believing the contrived story that befalls her when she is confronted with a series of bizarre deaths . . . Joe Eszterhas's screenplay manufactures red herrings by the shoal and offers more twists than you will find in a bowl of pretzels. In the end, though, it asks more questions than it answers and seems to exist merely to provide

Stone and Baldwin with a chance to indulge in some real heavy-duty bonking.

John Marriott didn't mince words in his review in the *Daily Mail*. He called it 'high-gloss embarrassment', and wrote:

> While claiming to seriously explore the ever-shifting line between reality and fantasy, and probe the pathological limits of voyeurism to boot, Eszterhas is clearly quite happy to chuck gravitas out the window and wallow in sex ... Suspense is spooned on with sledgehammer finesse. Unlike Hitchcock, who masterfully mounted his best thrillers block by block, and to whom Noyce paid tribute with *Dead Calm*, the director now blasts us from the off. ... As the thunder of the obvious swamps the film from the first frame to last, characters inhabit one dimension at best, and few real thrills emerge. Instead of blessing us with a character-driven mind game, with lessons to learn, both writer and director have attacked us with the garish gloss of a pop video and bolted on the ideas like an interfering sideshow. ... For those who haven't read *The Joy of Sex*, her [Stone's] extended workout with William Baldwin may provide the film's only lesson.

Hilary Bonner, of *Screen Mirror*, didn't think much of Sharon at all: 'Stone is glamorous and composed, totally confident in her screen allure but she is no actress, so any section in which she is speaking rather than posing or bonking are less than compelling. Berenger and Baldwin act around her, fleshing out rather insubstantial characters.'

Mark Salisbury in *Empire* had less of a critic's-eye view and more of a filmgoer's opinion:

> *Sliver* emerges as a film sadly lacking in both sauce and thrills, not a *bad* film exactly, just a clinical, inaccessible one, directed with impersonal efficiency by Phillip Noyce. The main problem lies with Joe Eszterhas's script which reworks themes from his own earlier efforts – *Basic Instinct*, *Jagged Edge*, *et al*

– as well as a good portion of Michael Powell's *Peeping Tom* into an incoherent tale about voyeurism and murder that trades on our expectations but does little to fulfil them.

Salisbury, who knew the problems which led to the film's new ending, wrote that the film's climax 'undermines all that's gone before'. He did, however, like Eszterhas 'gift for dialogue', but failed in 'trotting out another round of sexual clichés and murky intrigue, never once drawing back the protagonists' psyches and wasting endless possibilities offered by Zeke's prying pursuit.' This at least was one critic who gave some marks to Sharon Stone, 'an engagingly edgy heroine, better clothed than naked, but Baldwin's anonymous Zeke fails to convince as either a psycho, prince or pervert. Not awful, just dull.'

Film Review's Marianne Gray noted how the film had finally arrived 'with plenty of word of mouth – mostly bad and justifiably so because this is not a very good movie. The chemistry between Stone and paramour Billy Baldwin is so frigid it could cool a mortuary. The problem with *Sliver* is that it's a very good subject presented with tepid manipulation. . . . It's a real pity because the film looks great, the cast is strong, director Noyce has a history of good, taut thrillers, and producer Robert Evans is one of the studio system's strongest survivors.'

To a large extent, the reviews were not much worse than those for *Basic Instinct*, which still made pots of money. And although *Sliver* had proved somewhat disastrous at the home box office, it went on to take $78 million around the world. In fact, overseas it was more successful than the year's other 'biggies' – *A Few Good Men* and *In the Line of Fire*. Some may continue to argue that the film was not good enough to be a success in the US, but it seems more likely that its failure there was due more to moral outrage than anything else, since overseas – where people were less concerned with what Sharon was doing to whom than what she was doing on screen – *Sliver* was a big hit, giving the film a world gross of $114 million.

The version that was seen in Britain and the rest of Europe was the uncut version, complete with the masturbation scene that had been edited for American release. When Sharon learned that the

Brits would see her controversial bath scene intact, she said, 'I'm delighted it's going to be seen after all the effort and debate that went into it. It is probably the most honest view of private female behaviour in mainstream cinema. But the American censors seemed to run a mile from it. Maybe they thought it looked *too* real. But I can never guess how those in charge of film rating in America think about sex.'

More than likely, it was the world gross figure that saved Sharon Stone from disappearing completely. It also saved Joe Eszterhas. Over the next couple of years he went on to write *Showgirls* for Paul Verhoeven – their previous troubles forgotten – for a fee of around $3.5 million, and considering the outcome of *that* film, it might have been thought that Eszterhas had peaked, creatively and financially. But he still managed to get about $1 million for just the outline for *Jade*. By 1996 he was the most sought-after screenwriter in Hollywood, with numerous projects on the go, including a film about Mafia boss John Gotti and a thriller called *Reliable Sources* – his fee for both was around $3.5 million a piece – a film about soul singer Otis Redding which should net him around $1 million, *One Night Stand* for $3.5 million, and *Foreplay* which was said to have the potential to earn him as much as $10 million. He was also writing two pet projects, *Sacred Cow*, about an American President photographed in a compromising position with a cow, and *Layers of Skin*, the tale of a lesbian detective which sounded suspiciously like the premise Eszterhas had wanted to write to placate the gay protesters during the *Basic Instinct* controversy. One thing is certain; Sharon Stone would not be starring in that one.

In the fall of 1993 Sharon did a photographic spread for the German edition of *Vogue*, posing topless but covering her breasts with her hands, smoking a cigar and with what appeared to be a bizarre bulge in the crotch of her white Giorgio Armani men's shorts. Editor Anna Wintour said, 'Sharon is a great, glamorous movie star in an old-fashioned way, when so many actresses are anti that.'

The edition appeared in December, by which time she was well into production on *The Quick and the Dead*. For a while it looked as if the Western might never get made. TriStar were apparently nervous of giving it the green light because of the poor domestic takings of *Sliver*. Then the figures for the worldwide box office gave them some encouragement, but what they really wanted was a second major star to top-line *The Quick and the Dead*. During 1993, Gene Hackman – who that year won an Oscar as Best Supporting Actor for the already classic Western *Unforgiven* – performed in two other major Westerns, *Wyatt Earp* and *Geronimo*, and was considered by any studio as a major asset to any Western.

Sharon went after him to play Herod, but he turned her down: he had been very outspoken about screen violence and had only agreed to make *Unforgiven* when Clint Eastwood, star and director of that movie, persuaded him that the film was anti-violence. TriStar were eager to have Hackman on board for Sharon's film, and it was only when he eventually agreed to do it that they gave the final go-ahead. Production was planned for November 1993.

Meanwhile, Sylvester Stallone was heavily involved with setting up a film with producer Jerry Weintraub called *The Specialist*. They needed an actress to play a woman who hires an ex-CIA assassin to avenge the murder of her parents. Stallone and Weintraub agreed they needed 'a new Sharon Stone', and for six months they tried to find an actress to fit the bill.

Said Weintraub, 'Then one day I called Sly up and said, "Hey, what's wrong with the *old* Sharon Stone?" Sly thought about it, then laughed and said, "You know, you're right!" '

So why hadn't it occurred to them to approach the real Sharon Stone in the first place? They had, but with a Sylvester Stallone movie a second major star name was unnecessary, so while they wanted Sharon they preferred to find someone unknown who would not cost too much. Common sense finally prevailing over financial concerns, they went after Sharon. She read the script and decided that – while it still meant taking off her clothes and getting into some more heavy simulated sex, and while it was also basically an action film – it offered her a part unlike anything she had done before. So she signed a deal with Warner Brothers to follow *The Quick and the Dead* with *The Specialist*. It meant that she was fully employed right through production on *The Quick and the Dead* from November 1993 to February 1994, then straight into *The Specialist* from February until May: there would be no time to take a break in between the two movies.

The pre-production work on *The Quick and the Dead* took up much of her time and energy during the autumn of 1993. But she enjoyed her new-found power and said, with typical humour, 'It feels great to be a mogul. When I was a kid and said I was going to be an actress, everyone told me I was crazy. It took me thirteen years before I had a hit movie. It took a lot of willpower to keep working towards my dreams. I want to run the *entire* movie business. I'm in control at last!'

She worked closely with Sam Raimi on the overall look and design of the film. The town of Redemption was designed to look bleak and sinister, with the satanic house of Herod at the end of the main street. And the costumes were found by Sharon in Milan; they were said to be originals used by Italian film director Sergio Leone in his spaghetti Westerns *Once Upon a Time in the West* and *My Name is Nobody*.

She was working hard, fighting to get control of her own destiny. '*Sliver* was my big learning experience. I had the right to say no to all sorts of things in my contract, so I rolled over in an effort not to be difficult and be a good girl, and everything I rolled over on became the enormous errors of the picture. So I got to the point on *The Quick and the Dead* of fighting for everything: I'm not rolling over on this – it will not be *less* than this – it will *go* like this. I was very adamant that the quality of the piece be maintained.'

Among the battles she won was over how she should be dressed. She said:

Some people, who shall remain nameless, wanted me to wear a dress to ride into town. I thought, 'Oh yes, the gunslinger's going to ride into town side-saddle!' I mean, why not have her powder her nose before shooting the bad guy? They wanted a stereotype – and that made me so darned mad. There were some people who were concerned that there really weren't a lot of scenes for me to be naked in this movie, but, you know, there are a lot of ways to be sexy other than romping around naked. This character's not running around in the nude so she can get control over somebody.

They argued that the audience wouldn't know if she were a man or a woman. I told them, 'I think we've pretty permanently established my gender. I think that's an element we don't have to view as a mystery any more.' I don't think there's anyone who goes to see movies who doesn't know that Sharon Stone is a woman!

She also fought to have a scene cut from the script in which she was supposed to bed a young gunslinger, played in the film by teenage heart-throb Leonardo Di Caprio. She had nothing against the teenaged actor and said, 'Leonardo is a great talent and really good-looking and I think he will be one of the finest actors in decades.' But she felt that a sexy scene between the two of them would border on being 'paedophilic'. She said, 'He is a boy, not a man, and I'm a woman. I just felt it was wrong for me to have a huge sex scene with him. I had to take a stand, and am very relieved it was cut out of the script.'

Her one compromise to giving her character a sexier look was for her to wear tight leather trousers. 'It was a pleasure to keep my panties on. I mean, taking my clothes off is what I do at home in my spare time!'

Although she was co-producing the film, she had to fight Columbia-TriStar every inch of the way for what she wanted. Casting the film was not so difficult as they agreed on old-timers from Westerns of the past, Woody Strode – one of the first black stars of the 1960s remembered as one of *The Professionals* along with Lee Marvin, Burt Lancaster and Robert Ryan (although best remembered as the gladiator Draba in the epic *Spartacus*) – and Pat Hingle who co-starred in scores of films including *Hang 'Em High* with Clint Eastwood. It was Strode's last major film; he died shortly afterwards.

However, one piece of casting Sharon really had to fight for: her brother Michael. He had never acted before, but she wanted him to play a gunslinger. Since coming out of prison in 1980, he had worked hard, setting up his own marble and stone company. During his time behind bars and in his years of struggling to make a clean living, she gave him all the support and help he needed to keep him on the straight and narrow. He credited her with his success within the law, saying, 'I would still be in jail now if it hadn't been for Sharon.'

He admired her greatly for the way she had managed her career and reached the top of her profession, while he had to struggle to overcome drug addiction and a criminal record. 'I'm not bothered and I'm not bitter about her fame,' he said. 'I'm very proud to be her brother. Every one of her successes feels like my own.'

What he did have, though, was a growing desire to become an actor too. Now that she had some muscle, she decided to try to get him a part in *The Quick and the Dead*; but she had to win over the studio. 'They said, "Okay, we'll see him," ' said Sharon, 'but they kept putting it off until the bigger parts were cast.'

He had to audition along with all the other actors who wanted the part but, recalled Sharon, 'Michael came in and they went, "He's fabulous." '

Michael had not seen his son Brian since his marriage had broken down, and he had remained unmarried since divorcing. He was having to prove himself to everyone because of his shady past, and when he made his screen debut in *The Quick and the Dead*, he was enjoying something of a celebrity love affair with Olivia Newton-John's sister, Rona.

The strain of Sharon's media – and often negative – profile, the stress of making and then counting the takings of *Sliver*, and the sheer hard work of mounting her own production took its toll. 'By the time we were ready to make *The Quick and the Dead*, I didn't want to make it,' she said. 'I was just so worn out.'

Before heading off to the locations in Arizona, Sharon led the cast through a few days of rehearsal in Los Angeles. 'The night before the read-through of the script I was running a hundred and two fever. But by the time I left the rehearsal I was all right. We did all the fighting before we got to Arizona.'

The town of Redemption was constructed in Mescal, in the desert of Arizona. The cast and crew stayed at Tucson, fifty miles from the location, where Sharon rented a luxury adobe house.

The film had little in the way of plot, and was basically a series of gunfights. The challenge for Raimi was to find different ways to present the gunfights without them becoming repetitious. He said, 'There's a fine line between the cliché of previous Westerns and the classic aspects. Is the gunfight something that's so clichéd that audiences don't want to see it any more, or is it a classic element that has gone beyond the cliché and into myth? We wanted to bring a new edge in.'

Because the film belonged to a certain genre with a very black, almost fantastic slant to it – Sharon called it 'a new genre' – it was uncompromisingly violent. But Sharon defended this, saying, 'There's something about a period movie, and particularly a movie that's this kind of new genre, that takes the reality of the violence; it doesn't romanticize it.'

There were occasional discussions about cutting back on the violence, but Sharon enthusiastically raged, 'No! *More* violent. I want it *more* violent!'

Along with *Intersection*, the film was turning out to be the best filming experience Sharon had so far had. She said, 'When you go home from *Intersection* or from *The Quick and the Dead*, it's a nice day.'

She remained enthusiastic about the production two years later:

Every day I went to work was a nice day. Because I didn't have to fit in some element of femininity, I got to be *really* female; you know, a *real* woman. Look at the women in those old movies where they had all those unbelievable hairdos. I mean, excuse me, but just where did they get the cream rinse and curling iron? That's more a man's fantasy of what women should be like. There is rarely if ever a depiction of women as women really are.

I mean, even in contemporary films it's the same. When I go to see a movie with my girlfriends, I say, 'Do you do things like that girl did?' and none of them does. Women are portrayed according to a man's perspective. In *The Quick and the Dead* we were not paying homage to the man's view of Western women.

For one scene she had to spend ten days covered in mud. To keep relatively clean, she wore a wet suit under her costume and plastic bags on her feet to keep them dry. 'She's very unglamorous in this,' said Sharon's associate Judianna Makovsky, 'and that's the way she wanted it. Of course the studio wanted her to look good and we certainly didn't want her to pretend she wasn't feminine. The leather pants helped with that!'

She did at least have a kissing scene, with Tom Skerritt whom she subsequently described as 'the best kisser ever'. She even told him so. 'I showed up at his trailer and said, "You're the best kisser ever. You're so handsome and sexy and great and everything!" And he was like, "Great . . ." I closed the door and said, "I just wanted to tell you that, thanks," and left. And he was like, "Whaaaat?" '

Since her accident on a pony years before, she had avoided horses. Now that she was making a Western, there could be no further avoidance. Michael was well aware of the difficulty she had in overcoming her fear as she not only managed to get back in the saddle, but took to it with vigour. Riding became a passion in her life.

During filming the media managed to make mountains out of molehills. Sharon was said to have been convinced that a young British actress, Fay Masterson, who was playing a prostitute in the film, was upstaging her, and consequently had the script rewritten to make Fay's role much smaller. In typical Hollywood fashion, a so-called 'movie insider' said, 'It was pure jealousy on Sharon's part. She saw how talented Fay was and it worried her.'

The story sounded suspiciously like a ploy to restore Sharon's 'bad girl' image. Having been involved in the casting, it seemed inconceivable that she would get jealous just because a female member of the cast was talented. And there was little evidence to support the notion that she had become so paranoid as to presume that 20-year-old Fay was upstaging her. All of which, no doubt unfairly, served to cast the unwitting newcomer in a poor light. Said Fay, 'Sharon shouts a lot and is quite bossy. But I guess she's just trying to be professional.' And, of course, Sharon was pretty much the Boss, and yet even though she was co-producer, she did not have the kind of control over the production that would have allowed her to do what the so-called 'movie insider' alleged: 'She didn't confront Fay directly, but told the writers to cut out the bulk of her scenes. The woman practically rewrote the script.'

Considering that Sharon had to fight every inch to get the sex scene cut, to get her brother a role and to stop the studio from forcing her to turn on the sex appeal, she was not in a position to have the script rewritten once they were into production. The 'movie insider' was never named.

It was not the first time Sharon had been accused of throwing her weight around on a film set, and surprisingly she had reached a stage in her life where she really didn't mind the accusations. She said, 'Having the reputation of being a bitch makes people stay back a little, which gives me room to breathe.'

While filming progressed through Christmas and into the New Year, the relationship between her and Bill MacDonald finally came to a conclusion. Things had not been going well. Sharon wanted to marry Bill, but Naomi had refused to give him a divorce. Nevertheless, she was prepared to bide her time, and they were still living together. Then his name became linked to a criminal investigation for fraud. In Los Angeles, the Deputy District Attorney, Richard Lowenstein, said, 'There is a criminal investigation going on into a multi-million-dollar fraud case. No decision has been made on whether charges will be brought.' Yet again, an unnamed source, this time 'a friend', said, 'She's worried that Bill could face a scandal and arrest, and drag her career down with him.'

No charges were brought against him, but the prospect of an arrest and subsequent headlines could only add to an obviously distinct cooling-off in the romance, due in no small part to the ongoing media attention to what was still considered an act of 'homewrecking'. 'I was living with my boyfriend at the time,' Sharon said, 'and I moved into my own room.'

Finally Bill moved out of the house in Tucson and went back to Los Angeles. Shortly after, he received Sharon's engagement ring, sent by Federal Express: the break was complete and quick.

Subsequently, Sharon said, 'I now accept that I don't have a private life. I'm not a kid on dates and demand too little from a man to be really interesting. I have my own life, career, independence and money, so the things that women typically seem to need from a man, I'd not need.' However, there was a new man in her life before the end of filming: assistant director Bob Wagner, almost ten years younger than she was.

During the filming of *The Quick and the Dead*, Roman Polanski announced that he was planning a remake of Luis Buñuel's 1967 erotic classic *Belle de Jour*, and that he wanted Sharon Stone to star. She would, he hoped, play the role created by Catherine Deneuve as a virginal newlywed who, unbeknownst to her husband, works the day shift in a high-class Parisian brothel. Said Polanski, 'Sharon Stone is a great actress and she has the perfect body for the film. That is a rare combination in an actress. She is perfect for the part.'

Sadly, the idea came to nothing, either because Sharon just didn't want to do another erotic film or simply because Polanski wasn't able to get his idea for the remake off the ground, but she would have been delighted to know that a director of such esteem, despite his notoriety, had publicly praised her, not just for her looks but for her acting.

The Quick and the Dead wrapped in February 1994. She had to leave the editing to Raimi, return to Los Angeles for just a week to deal with some business, then head off to Miami, Florida, for her date with Sylvester Stallone. Finishing her Western, she reflected, 'I've had some lean, difficult times. And after all the excitement, hype and fame, doing *The Quick and the Dead* brought me back to centre. I don't make choices now for the public.'

10

Specializing With Sly

Again it was going to be a long schedule, but at least *The Specialist* was being filmed in the comfort and sunshine of Miami. To all intents, this was a 'Sylvester Stallone movie', full of powerful and often violent action. Like Arnold Schwarzenegger, Stallone had become firmly fixed in the minds of the public as an action man with almost indestructible qualities. Yet he had begun his career – after a couple of forgettable films – with a particulary fine performance as *Rocky* which he also scripted. For this he was Oscar-nominated both as Best Actor and for Best Screenplay. The success of that film meant a sequel was inevitable, followed by several more, all of which served to dilute the quality of the original and helped critics and public to forget that Stallone was an action man who could *act*.

Playing Rambo in three films consolidated his position as an heroic box-office star, but – desperate to break away from type – he had a disastrous attempt at comedy in *Stop, Or My Mom Will Shoot*, and finally accepted that if he was to remain a success, he had to return to the genre that people preferred him in. So he made *Cliffhanger*, which called for him to do little more than be physical. It had a definite tongue-in-cheek approach which was even more evident in the comic-strip antics of *Demolition Man* and was later taken to extremes in *Judge Dredd*. In between *Cliffhanger* and *Judge Dredd*, he wanted a film he hoped would be the kind in which the public liked him, but which would also offer him something different to do. He said, '*The Specialist* is not just an action film. This movie is a foray into a genre that I've been longing to do for a long time – an erotic thriller. There's a great deal of difference between an action film and an erotic thriller. Obviously, I've kind of digressed at times and gone into comedy and lost audiences when I did it. The comedies I tried didn't work. Throughout my career I've tried – I've really tried. I've tried to take chances and I find there's usually resistance.'

He was, in fact, talking of the very thing Joe Eszterhas had warned Sharon about when he said that she should not try to play anything different. Said Stallone about his own lesson:

Usually in everyday situations I consider myself rather more humorous. I enjoy the absurd very much. But the comedies I have done have not done very well. Either that's my failure or, more importantly, I think that the vehicle itself wasn't really suited to my personality. I think maybe comedy is best left to comedians and I'll stick with what I'm doing. I tried and the main thing is I learned from failure.

Certain actors become like a product, and when you go to a movie you expect a certain kind of result. The message I get is, 'If I want to see a comedy I'll go and see Steve Martin – I don't want to see you. From you I expect something else.' And that's always Rocky, Rambo, Cobra. They relate to that.

This is what I am – why not make the best of it? I think I do fairly well in this genre. I understand it and I like the danger. I like the challenge it provides. Once you come to terms with something, once you accept what you are, where things are, then there's no real conflict.

That was a philosophy Sharon was fighting hard to beat. She had said that she was no longer making choices for the public, and she would continue to do that. But whether or not she would succeed in breaking the mould, as Stallone had failed to do, remained to be seen. But then Stallone, unlike Sharon, *was* making choices for the public.

In *The Specialist* Stallone at least came to a compromise, satisfying his own desire to do something more dramatic as well as the studio's insistence that he still came across as an action man. Studios – and sadly the public, and even the critics – had forgotten that Stallone had proved himself to be an actor capable of giving a dramatic performance with depth and conviction, as with the first *Rocky*, and then later in *Paradise Alley*. 'That film didn't get recognition,' he said, 'but it is the best I think I have ever acted in. *Cliffhanger* was a very, very important film but it wasn't what I would call a real acting performance. You go through the motions. It was more of a physical display. But with *The Specialist* you have to pull it out because 80 per cent of it is looks and emotions, and it has to come out in the eyes. If you're really thinking about the situation, it comes across in your acting. If you're thinking about your lines and hitting your marks, then you're mediocre.'

In this film he played a CIA 'specialist' who, with his immediate superior, played by James Woods, carried out covert operations for the government, which includes assassination. But Stallone has a conscience, and when a murder results in the death of a child, he attacks Woods and disappears.

Years later Stallone, working as a killer-for-hire, is sought by Sharon Stone who is looking for someone to avenge the deaths of her parents. Stallone takes his time meticulously checking her out before accepting the assignment, but he misses the fact that the woman is working with Woods, who wants his own vengeance on Stallone.

Sharon's role again featured nudity and sex, but at least she felt this offered some good, solid dramatic elements. On the set of the film she told *Empire*'s Jeff Dawson, 'For fifteen years I made a lot of crap, and I worked really hard. I have a very simple blue-collar work ethic – I like to have a job and I like to be part of a team. I just get to pick better things now.'

Stallone certainly hoped for better things from this film. Of it, and of Sharon, he said:

This time I'm dealing with the erotic side of my personality. I play a man who lives in the shadows – he's a mysterious character. Even though he's an assassin of sorts, he has an extraordinary code. But the movie is more about the man leading a voyeuristic life, and this relationship he develops with Sharon Stone. He begins to do business with her over the phone. Her family was killed years ago and she wants revenge for that. He doesn't want to work with her because he feel's something's wrong, but the way she speaks to him is so seductive. He becomes enamoured and he follows her. He goes into her apartment. He immerses himself so deeply in her psyche that when he finally meets her it's an erotic explosion.

Sharon Stone is a big asset. For this kind of film, Sharon is *it* – the actress I would most want to act with. She has this genre, this particular mood covered, so I guess I made the right choice.

There were those who were expecting a clash of huge egos, but from the outset Stone and Stallone were locked into a warm friendship. In fact, said Stallone, the whole production turned out to be the smoothest of his career. It tended to become something of a mutual admiration society for Sharon and Sly. She said, 'Sly's great. He's totally professional, very talented and – what a lot of people don't seem to realize – very, very smart.'

The cast included Rod Steiger playing a Cuban crime lord, and Eric Roberts as his psychotic son who had been responsible for the death of Stone's parents. For Steiger, who had suffered from clinical depression for years and been all but forgotten by Hollywood, this was a comeback which he thoroughly relished, even though he spent most of the film in considerable pain, having just had a hip replacement: the walking-stick he used was not a mere prop. He referred to his fellow-actors on the set with gentlemanly grace: *Mr* Stallone, *Miss* Stone, *Mr* Woods.

From him 'Miss Stone' learned more about the pitfalls of Hollywood. Steiger had won an Oscar for his performance in the 1967 classic *In the Heat of the Night*. On the set of *The Specialist* he told how he recently went to see 'one of the 3,000 Vice Presidents at one of the studios' who was 'a kid' in his thirties. 'Can you do a Southern accent?' asked the executive.

'I won an Academy Award doing a Southern accent in a film called *In the Heat of the Night*,' answered Steiger. 'Did you ever see it?'

'No!' the studio executive replied.

Steiger said *that's* when he realised that 'these pseudo studio executives' didn't know who he was, and he needed to find a way to remind them. 'This picture is a Godsend. I couldn't ask for a better commercial.'

Perhaps it was the ever-warm Miami sunshine, or the luxury of the Biltmore Hotel where the principals were accommodated, or just a mixing of like minds, but Sharon too found the film one of the most enjoyable she had ever done. 'Sly is just hilarious,' she said. 'He tells jokes and makes everybody laugh. He makes it really fun. It's great.'

In March, when Sharon returned to Hollywood to be at the Oscars, she turned up with a man nobody could identify. The columnists almost went mad trying to put a name to him, and she enjoyed herself immensely teasing the press who wanted to know who was the new stranger in her life. It turned out to be brother Michael, whose face was still new to the media.

Returning to Miami, there were to be a couple of sexy scenes for Sharon and Sly to share – one in bed, the other in the shower. Sharon seemed more at ease in stripping off than Stallone did. She said, 'I'm 36 and in five years I won't be this hot thing any more. But I have a feeling my brain will stay where it is for a while.' As always, she consulted her father before embarking on the nude scenes. He told her, 'As long as you keep your pride.'

Stallone was very protective about her nude scenes; the world's paparazzi had descended on Miami at the news that Sharon Stone was about to reveal all again. Knowing that advance photographs of her in the shower would be eagerly sought by any means possible, he brought in extra security to keep cunning photographers right away from the tightly closed set. There was also the threat of immediate dismissal for any member of the film crew caught helping a photographer. There were no incidents, and the smooth running of the production continued.

Stallone was adamant that only a handful of essential crew members would be on set for the steamy shower scene. One of the crew reckoned, 'He definitely had a thing about his butt. He figured the guys would trade a few stories around the bars if he humped Sharon in full view of everyone. So he had Luis Llosa, the director, do the scene behind closed doors.'

Certainly Stallone's muscular buttocks were featured more prominently than Sharon's in the final cut; perhaps Llosa felt the world would prefer an alternative view for once. Whatever was in the director's mind, Jerry Weintraub said, 'I have never seen anything so erotic, so sensual or so sexy in my life.' He thought that Stallone reminded him of a young Jean-Paul Belmondo, while 'Sharon is everything she was in *Basic Instinct.*'

Stallone said of the scenes, 'They are the most sensual I have ever done. Sharon is everything you see in her films. She's beautiful, very sexy and smart.'

He also joked that in the bedroom scene, he was not giving Sharon the dominant position on top just so that the camera could dwell on her figure. 'I'm not Michael Douglas!' he quipped in reference to the *Basic Instinct* scene in which Sharon is on top with Douglas underneath. 'I don't function well on the bottom! I like to move and I like the view. I don't want the basement apartment!'

Sadly for the more voyeuristic, what finally emerged on film did not quite live up to its reputation, although Sharon had probably been glad that the sex scenes were toned down. For her, the film was a chance to be dramatic more than seductive. But she had not lost her sense of humour; she said, 'In this film I'm just a cheap coke whore slut mean vixen. It's a *blast!*'

She had her own security guard, who had worked for President Nixon. When Nixon died that May, the guard apparently asked for time off to attend the funeral. In time-honoured Hollywood tradition, the story that emerged had it that Sharon told him that if he went, he could forget his job. That version was easy to swallow if one considered Sharon Stone to be the heartless bitch she had sometimes been painted to be, but it just didn't fit in with the purposely maintained low profile of her time spent at Camp Unity in Los Angeles, cooking for homeless children. Some sceptics may have accused Sharon of putting on a display of charity to give her image a boost, but she was of course heavily involved in charity work long before she began getting a bad press.

She had also said, 'The upside of all this *famous* mularkey is that it gives you an opportunity to meet people for whatever reason – not just so you can settle down and have kids, which I want to do, but so you can become involved in the worldwide scheme, like social politics, where you can help causes and effectively push for changes.' She may have sounded a little like Dorothy gushing at the end of *The Wizard of Oz*, but it should be remembered that these were the sort of ethics with which she and her brothers and sister had been brought up.

As regards the security guard, he did go to Nixon's funeral, but he didn't come back. It was said that Sharon fired him; she insisted that he had resigned.

The nude scenes certainly gave both Sly and Sharon the chance to show off their fine physiques. Five years earlier, there were stories that Stallone had been taking steroids which had made his muscles bigger than ever. It was said he had been damaging his body, and he had sworn off using steroids again. Consequently, by 1994 and at the age of 47, he was relying solely on exercise – and while still incredibly muscular, he looked relatively trimmer.

As for Sharon, she was looking thinner. She said, 'People thought I lost weight for the film, but I'm not thinner. I think my body is changing. My face is changing. I don't know if it's because of getting older or because I work so much.' She added, 'I am tired all the time.'

Her stamina was at an all-time low, and in an attempt to get her into good shape, Warner Brothers provided her with a personal fitness trainer. They thought she was being a good girl and getting her daily workout, but she admitted, 'I don't have time to work out. They pay for a trainer and I pretend that I am using her. But if I do anything I end up getting a massage.'

During filming, she was approached to portray the legendary movie star Marlene Dietrich in a film scripted by Louis Malle, based on the book by Dietrich's daughter, Maria Riva. The book had not proved quite the *Mommie Dearest* assassination-type job many had expected, but it nevertheless revealed much about the star that was less than savoury, as Riva made every effort to put the record straight while trying not to tarnish the basic image Dietrich's fans cherished. It was a proposition Sharon seriously considered. Later, Uma Thurman was said to have been cast as Dietrich. But when Louis Malle died shortly thereafter, the project died with him.

Although the emphasis on Sharon's role in *The Specialist* wasn't sex, it nevertheless featured her as a woman who uses her sexuality to achieve her own ends, even to the point of bedding the man she wants dead in a scene which had her and Eric Roberts in bed for a week. 'I wouldn't call it a love scene, I wouldn't call it sex,' she explained. 'It was very perverse! I'm motivated through the picture to kill him so it's a very perverse seduction that she gets into, hating him while she's grappling with him. It's very tough and weird, like I'm in a black dress, drunk, smoking cigarettes.' Of the actor concerned, Eric Roberts, she said, 'He's so beautiful, like a Michelangelo dream.'

Again, the scene was cut (mainly because the studio didn't want the film to get an NC-17 rating), although Eric Roberts fondly remembered his week in bed with Sharon, saying, 'The funny thing about it was, here's Sharon with her right breast exposed all day long. *All day long!*'

During filming, it was reported that Sly had become a father again. He already had two teenage sons by his first wife, Sasha; but the new arrival in Stallone's life was not one he celebrated. Engaged to Jennifer Flavin for some years, he had managed to weave something of a tangled web for himself by getting involved with model Janice Dickinson some months prior to filming *The Specialist*. It turned out she was pregnant, and it was reported that consequently he dumped Jennifer to be with Janice. While he was in Miami filming with Sharon Stone, Janice gave birth to a baby girl, Savannah Rodin. Stallone – the 'proud father', as reports described him – promptly set up a trust fund for the baby.

When she was able to travel, Janice went to Miami to meet Stallone, where they discussed marriage. He insisted she sign a pre-nuptial agreement, which she rejected, and she demanded he make massive support payments. The argument ended when Sly took back a Mercedes he had given to her, and she returned to Los Angeles.

The outcome of all this was a DNA test which finally proved that Stallone wasn't the father, and some time later Jennifer took him back. In 1996 she gave him his own real baby daughter, Sophia Rosa. With his personal crisis coming right in the middle of filming, the media concentrated on him, leaving Sharon relatively undisturbed to carry on her relationship with Bob Wagner. For once, she was able to relinquish much of her responsibility for promoting the film, as Stallone occupied the majority of the media attention. He said:

> Every other poster I see is a Rambo rip-off, a guy holding a weapon – Steven Seagal, Chuck Norris, Arnold, Van Damme. I just said, 'It's time for you to move on,' and with this film it's more suspenseful. More Hitchockian.
>
> I haven't really done much true acting in fifteen years. The kind of movies I've been making have relied more on action and stunts than acting. That's why I enjoyed making this film. For once it's my character, not the action, that is important. I get to *act* – show some depth to the guy with sensitivity.'

Not that the film was in any way short on action. Playing a character who is an expert in explosives meant that Stallone's acting was always being interrupted by a variety of explosions, some small, some big and some quite monumental – such as when the whole of Stallone's secret home self-destructs in the film's final scene.

Despite all the pyrotechnics and stunt work, Stallone kept the attention focused on the other qualities of the film. 'It's more of a *feminine* film, and that's what I'm going for,' he said. 'And when I say feminine, it has softer edges. It isn't guys jumping through windows and who can take the most punches – and that for me works.'

Sadly, much of Stallone's effort to keep the dramatic qualities of the film was later lost in the cutting. He was bothered by the scene in which he finally kills Eric Roberts, set at an exclusive Miami hotel. Stallone, in tennis outfit and carrying a racket that turns out to be a transmitter, sits by the pool waiting for the tea-trolley on its way to Eric Roberts in the hotel lobby. All Stallone has to do is place his cunning exploding teacup and saucer on the trolley, take his seat by the pool and, using his equally cunning tennis racket, detonate the bomb. The blocking was simple, giving Stallone cause to try to find something more interesting to do. The camera rolled, Stallone swung his racket, sat down on a sun-lounger and ogled the women in swim-suits. Cut! Llosa was pleased, Stallone wasn't. They tried again. Once more Stallone was dissatisfied.

He and Llosa got together with the on-set script editor and Stallone came up with a single line which he used in the next take, saying, 'Hey, is this seat free?' before he sat down. He hoped it would add to the cool demeanour of the character as he prepares to blow up part of the hotel. While in editing, the line disappeared. . . .

In the scene Stallone sees Sharon Stone walking into the lobby, but he is unable to stop the ensuing explosion. It was an easy take for the director. Then came the explosion itself, with Roberts and Stone evacuating the set while two stunt men took up their places as two bodyguards about to get blown to pieces. Hotel guests, unable to use the pool that day, gathered to watch the shot. The special effects were rigged so that the hotel would actually remain undamaged by the controlled explosion, but there was always the chance – as in any stunt like this – that things could go wrong.

The special effects director gave the countdown, the button was pressed and the hotel seemed to blow up in what appeared on film as a mighty explosion. Out of the smoke walked the two stunt men to applause from the gathered crowd, the crew and the actors, and somewhere the hotel manager was taking a deep breath of relief that his hotel was still standing.

Despite the later critical backlash the film would receive, it was something of a dramatic deviation for Sly who dominated the whole thing, not just with his physique – which remains a vital tool of his trade – but with his moody persona. Though not quite the dramatic breakthrough both stars had hoped for, the film has a brooding inevitability about it which director Luis Llosa maintains throughout the whole first half of the film, particularly while the script keeps Stallone and Stone apart. It is only when Stallone takes on the job of killing Eric Roberts that it becomes another, albeit superior, action film. When Stallone and Stone get together it tried hard to be the erotic thriller Stallone had hoped for, but thankfully the sex scenes are brief and dull. But in all the film generated a smouldering, brooding atmopshere, beautifully bound up by John Barry's equally brooding score.

As for Sharon, however it may have looked in the original script, what reached the screen was a film that belonged solely to Stallone. Nevertheless, she is persuasive as a woman with vengeance on her mind who has no real scruples as to how she gets it, thus setting up Stallone for his potential come-uppance at the hands of James Woods, who is superbly psychotic. Roberts is fine too, and only Rod Steiger jars with his old-style hammy acting.

The film finished in the early summer. Stallone remained in Miami, where he had bought himself a white-brick-fronted estate in the Coconut Grove area. Sharon returned to Los Angeles.

Intersection was finally released in 1994, and panned by the critics, although Sharon got some good personal notices. 'It sounds really obnoxious,' she said, 'but I got *great* reviews, so I felt pretty good about it. They hate the film, but they *loved* me.'

Empire called it 'a drab, glossy remake of a French psychological drama where comatose Richard Gere hovers between life and death, while struggling on the horns of a dilemma, torn between his perfect wife, Sharon Stone, and his passionate mistress, Lolita Davidovich. The whole thing is doomed since the trio's agonizing – so deep and meaningful in French – is plain tedious in English.' *Screen Mirror* thought the film 'an interesting idea with the drama taking place during a developing car accident. Flashbacks relate to the incidents in each of the victims' lives that led to this critical moment ... Sharon Stone, the former femme fatale of film, covers up to play a wife and mother.'

Despite the film's panning by critics, Sharon worked hard to promote it, and throughout it all she was like a chameleon, cleverly adapting to the readership or audience she was addressing. Interviewed by the *New York Times*, she surprised the readers by

letting them know she could talk intelligently about art and literature. She played 'the movie queen' by allowing herself to be photographed draped across a grand piano for a film magazine. She
posed topless for *Vanity Fair*, but says she was conned into doing
that. When David Letterman interviewed her on his TV chat show,
she charmed him and the audience with her humour as she wildly
flirted with him on air. She also appeared on TV with the eminent
Barbara Walters, and turned up on *Good Morning America* wearing
a pink bathrobe.

Intersection managed to take only a modest $33 million. At this
point, Joe Eszterhas's prediction that Sharon would be making a
mistake in trying to do different kinds of roles seemed to be proving accurate. Although she couldn't save the film, she did a lot to
salvage her public image after all the mud-slinging over her relationship with Bill MacDonald.

In July 1994, she was seen at the élite Chateau Marmont Hotel,
frolicking in the pool with (apparently) Keanu Reeves. New York
reporter Allan Hall quoted an 'onlooker' as saying, 'It was like they
were choreographed in the pool. There was some serious tonsil
massaging going on. On a scale of one to ten, if they were lovers, I'd
put them around 78!'

There were, however, no photographers to back up the story, and
if the two stars were indeed enjoying a brief fling, then *brief* was the
operative word. As far as all her friends knew, she was still with Bob
Wagner. He was living with her in her house, and as she began to
think more and more about having children, she told friends that
she thought Bob would make an ideal father. But the word was that
Sharon was growing impatient with Bob's apparent lack of ambition; he seemed content to live with her in her house and allow her
to supply him with work.

That summer she began receiving threatening phone calls; then
her house was broken into without the alarms going off. Keanu
Reeves was said to be comforting her, although no one was saying
where Bob Wagner was supposed to be at this time; but certainly
Sharon was sufficiently terrified to hire herself a team of Israeli
bodyguards recommended by Elizabeth Taylor, who entrusted her
own life to them.

After spending months of filming and then promoting, Sharon was exhausted and decided she needed time off to paint, sculpt, ride her horse Magic, and look for property away from Hollywood. 'I need to get out,' she said.

But there were still decisions to be made. Playing Marlene Dietrich certainly appealed to her; so did the idea of remaking the Marilyn Monroe classic *Niagara* which was put to her. For a long time she had been trying to establish herself in her own right. She was a genuine film fan and knew all about the great Hollywood movie queens; she had wanted to be counted among them ever since she was a little girl. Although the likes of Dietrich and Monroe had come from a different era, she understood something of the pressures they faced, both professionally and privately: if anything, Sharon and her generation of movie queens had it much harder than those from the so-called Golden Days of Hollywood. Yesterday's movie stars had the studios looking out for them, cultivating them, giving them security even if the price was often a case of selling their souls.

The old star system discovered women like Dietrich and Monroe and, recognizing the qualities that made these people potential stars, gave them the screen vehicles to realize their potential. Sharon had had to do all this herself, and it had taken her a long time while most of her peers achieved stardom at an earlier age. 'I worked really hard then because I was pulling such a heavy load when the films weren't good,' she said, 'and you *knew* they weren't going to be any good.'

So while she understood the problems the earlier screen legends had, she was fascinated by the system that had made them what they were. And she was also fascinated by the personalities, which was why she had wanted to do *The Immortals*. However, because she did not want to impersonate Monroe – she knew she could *not* impersonate her – she finally had to turn it down. But to play a role that Monroe had herself played, as in *Niagara*, she could allow herself an element of fantasy by sharing something in common with the undeniably greatest movie queen ever.

But if she had been hesitant about portraying the real Monroe, she had fewer qualms about portraying Dietrich. Perhaps she felt that too many had tried to portray Monroe – among them Catherine Hicks and Melanie Anderson – while nobody had attempted a serious portrayal of Dietrich. The project became one for Chaos Productions to consider. It may have been that Sharon was just so worn out at the time that it didn't get off the ground – the *Niagara* remake was also still grounded – but her fascination with the lives of her predecessors and remakes of classic films did not abate.

There was now, it seemed, something of a crisis in Sharon's career, which no doubt affected her earlier decision to take a year off. Then she heard about a film Martin Scorsese was making, and she decided she had to do it.

11

'Marty! Marty! Marty!'

Martin Scorsese had literally come from the mean streets that inspired many of his films, including *Mean Streets* and *GoodFellas*. He grew up in New York's tough 'Little Italy' neighbourhood where the Mafia were much in evidence during the 1940s. Although his own parents were clean-living and hard-working, his best friend's father was a genuine mobster. Of those early days, he recalled:

It was a very closed-off community where the main authority was organized crime. Gangsters were the first people I knew. The older men were very nice, but some of the younger wise guys were mean. You saw them beat up people. Bang! Suddenly there's a baseball bat and someone's on the ground. Some close friends of mine tried to be wise guys, but it takes a kind of immorality. If you're a foot soldier, you have to be able to kill somebody. Can you do that? The secret was to be respectful, be polite and remember that they are bloodsuckers. Some of my friends flirted with it, but they turned out to be good people.

It was these memories that prompted him to explore the dark, and sometimes not so dark, side of the underworld when he turned to directing films. *GoodFellas*, set during the 1960s, was, at its time of release, the most authentic and uncompromising screen portrait of Mafia life ever filmed. In 1994 Scorsese was preparing to film not a follow-up but another relatively modern portrait of organized crime, this time set during the 1970s. It was called *Casino*.

This was based on a true story and put into book form by Nicholas Pileggi, who interested Scorsese in filming it by showing him a newspaper article about what was little more than a domestic fight that took place on a lawn in Las Vegas one Sunday morning. The police were called and a ten-year history, which culminated in the domestic on the lawn, began to unravel.

Scorsese was intrigued to find what he described as 'this incredible story with so many tangents, and each is one more nail in their coffin'. The history involved Carl DeLuna, the underboss of Kansas City, who was always complaining that he had to spend his own money on his trips to Las Vegas and was never reimbursed. Back in Kansas, there was a homicide which prompted the police to bug DeLuna and thereby alert the FBI to various names linked to Las Vegas casinos, including Frank 'Lefty' Rosenthal, his wife Geri and Tony Spilotro. 'I just thought it would be a terrific story,' said Scorsese, who sat down with Nicholas Pileggi and began writing the screenplay of *Casino*.

In the process they had to change various names and, in the terms the lawyers insisted on, say 'the film was adapted from a true story' as opposed to 'this film is based on a true story'. Frank 'Lefty' Rosenthal became Sam 'Ace' Rothstein, Geri became Ginger, and Tony Spilotro became Nicky Santoro. Dramatic license was also taken with various locations, so that some things that actually happened in Chicago are depicted as occurring in Vegas.

The screen story that evolved was a complex saga covering ten years, from 1973 to 1983. The original draft of the script began with the domestic on the lawn between 'Ace' and Ginger. 'We realized the story structure was too detailed and didn't create enough dramatic satisfaction at the end of the picture,' Scorsese explained. 'So Nick and I decided to start the film with the car exploding, seeing

"Ace" Rothstein go up into the air in slow motion, flying over the flames – like a soul about to take a dive into hell!'

Following this murder of 'Ace' in 1983, the film takes a flashback to ten years earlier when he is entrusted by the mob to oversee the Tangiers casino in Las Vegas. His specific job is to manage an operation by which money is skimmed from the counting room and delivered to Kansas City. The official casino manager is Phillip Green, but it is 'Ace' who turns the place into a huge success.

He falls for a hooker, Ginger, who becomes his mistress, although she still has feelings for her former boyfriend, pimp Lester Diamond. Ginger marries 'Ace', and he places $2 million in a Los Angeles bank as security in case of kidnapping, giving her the only key. The mob sends a hitman, Nicky Santoro, to Vegas to protect 'Ace', and before long Nicky sets up his own racket to provide extra profits to the bosses. He finally manages to get himself blacklisted from every Vegas casino, and sets up a new operation with his brother Dominic, effectively beginning a reign of terror.

Ginger asks 'Ace' to give her $25,000, but refuses to tell him why she needs it; Lester Diamond has asked her for it. Nicky follows Ginger to her rendezvous with Diamond and beats him up. Despite a long-time friendship, relations between 'Ace' and Nicky deteriorate, and Ginger indulges in alcohol and drugs. 'Ace's' problems increase when local commissioner Pat Webb instigates an investigation by the Gaming Control Board into 'Ace' himself and the Tangiers casino. The bosses urge him to lie low, but instead he decides to host an in-house TV show.

Ginger tells him she wants a divorce, and when he refuses to give her one, she takes her jewels and their daughter Amy to Los Angeles, where she plans to take off with Lester Diamond. But Nicky gets to her and brings her back to Vegas. Later, when she asks Nicky to help her to get her jewellery which has been confiscated by 'Ace', the two begin an affair.

Eventually Ginger manages to leave 'Ace', and gets the $2 million from the bank. The mob bosses, realizing that the FBI are about to shut down the Tangiers and arrest all involved, arrange for a series of deaths. Nicky plants a bomb in 'Ace's' car but, miraculously, he survives. Later Nicky and his brother are beaten to death in the desert with baseball bats. The Tangiers is destroyed and the other mob-run casinos are transformed into theme parks. Ginger dies from an overdose of drink and drugs, and 'Ace' goes to San Diego where he sets himself up as a successful bookie.

When it came to the question of casting, there was no one else to play the part of 'Ace' Rothstein other than Robert De Niro. Few other actors, if any, have ever been able to give the sort of portrayal of mobsters that Scorsese has always striven for, mixing the ruthless traits of such characters with gentler elements to win the audience's sympathy. This De Niro achieved best of all in, not a Scorsese film but a Sergio Leone film, *Once Upon a Time in America*, in which he was a lifelong criminal who killed and raped, and yet managed to come across before the closing credits as a sympathetic character. He did the same again in Scorsese's *GoodFellas*, although it would be true to say that Scorsese took a more harsh, less romantic approach. The same was true also of *Casino*.

Said Scorsese, 'Very often the people I portray can't help but be in that way of life. Yes, they're bad. And we condemn those aspects of them. But they're also human beings, and I find that often the people passing moral judgment on them may ultimately be worse.' He had seen the actual photographs of the bodies of the men featured in the film as Nicky and his brother. 'Nicky is horrible,' said Scorsese. 'He's a terrible man. But there's something that happens to me in watching them get beaten with the bats and then put into the hole. Ultimately it's a tragedy. It's the frailty of being human. I want to push audiences' emotional empathy with certain types of character who are normally considered villains.'

This, of course, has been true of every gangster film made since Edward G. Robinson was *Little Caesar*, James Cagney was *Public Enemy* and Paul Muni was *Scarface*. But with the boundaries of screen violence pushed even further back – perhaps questionably so – by the 1990s, Scorsese was able to show the terrible truths about such men yet *still* capture the audience's sympathy. This is in no small part due to the screen persona of Robert De Niro because, despite the fact that he happens to be Scorsese's favourite actor, he has become accepted by audiences in these roles. It becomes easier for the director to establish the character as one the audience will care about enough to sit through three hours of his story.

'We've come to know each other fairly well over the years,' Scorsese told *Empire*'s Philip Thomas about his long association with De Niro, 'and he has an interesting side to him. He's a very compassionate man. He's basically a very good man, and you can see that in him. So he can take characters who are pretty disturbing and make them human because of that compassion. He has that ability to make an audience feel empathy for very difficult characters because there's something very decent about him.'

Another of Scorsese's favourite actors, Joe Pesci, was easily cast as Nicky Santoro, and James Woods as Lester Diamond. Of course, De Niro, Pesci and Scorsese had worked together in *Raging Bull* and *GoodFellas*, but with the addition this time of James Woods, Scorsese had, perhaps consciously, reunited the principals of Leone's *Once Upon a Time in America*. What he needed next was the perfect Ginger. It was said that every leading lady in Hollywood wanted the part; that may have been an exaggeration, but there's no doubt that it was a sought-after role. Among those seeking it was Sharon Stone.

She had long wanted to co-star with Robert De Niro, whom she considered one of America's finest actors. She also wanted to work with one of America's finest directors, Scorsese. 'You always want to work with the finest people – the very best people. And that is what I had in *Casino*. One of my goals had always been to be good enough to work with Robert De Niro.'

But more than that, she wanted to play Ginger. 'I had been playing typical, very superficial female roles. I'm soon going to be too old to play those parts. Actress years are like dog years, so I'm about 166! But this was a character who had much more range than anything else I had done. It was based on a real person, so it was an actual life-experience. It had truth. I had to play it.'

Sharon got her agent to approach Scorsese, and understandably he was at first unconvinced that she was an actress with enough depth to carry the role. 'She really wanted the job,' said Scorsese. 'She is a very formidable lady.' She was also very shrewd; she said that if she got the part, she would do it for just a nominal fee. So he arranged for a meeting. He recalled, 'After I first met her, I knew she undoubtedly had a presence, but I didn't know if she would have the ability to do the movie.'

He arranged for De Niro to meet her, and said, 'I wanted to see if they got along together. She had to be uninhibited, lash out at Bob and fly into an uncontrollable rage.' When they ran through the lawn argument scene, Sharon made sure she did not hold back. Said Scorsese, 'Some movie stars won't let that extra part of them be exposed. She did – and she was great.'

Scorsese felt that in Sharon's favour was a resemblance to Ginger – or rather Geri. 'Same stature, same blonde hair and blue eyes,' said the director. He also believed that her relatively new arrival on the scene was an advantage. 'Sharon had been knocking around Hollywood for years,' he said, 'just like Ginger had been kicking around Las Vegas. But Sharon had only just become a big movie star even though she had been in the business for ages. It was that quality I wanted.'

And so Sharon, without any fee to speak of – certainly nothing like the millions she was used to getting – got to play Ginger. She also got Bob Wagner a job, as an assistant director.

Several days of rehearsals began in October in Las Vegas, where the bulk of the film would be shot over a period of four months. 'I think I started in a state of abject terror and I could hardly speak,' Sharon told *Film Review*'s Edward Peterborough. 'Then I snapped out of that in short order and started throwing myself at them until they had no choice.'

The problem Sharon faced was the fact that Scorsese, De Niro and Pesci were old friends and a professional team; she was the newcomer, and hardly one of the men! For her, is was like being excluded from an exclusive boys' club.

At first I felt like a potted plant. Marty would talk about the scene to the boys, and I was sort of left standing on the side-lines. I was just trailing around after him going, 'Marty! Marty! Marty!' until he turned around and said, 'What do you want?' We were just fine after that.

I found working with Marty was an organic sort of experi-ence. Usually on a film, you get the script, you show up on

time and you shoot it. You're having to work at it as you do it.
But with Marty he rehearses and works to a sort of rhythm by
which he begins where you get the material, you sit down with
it, then you find the voice of the characters, and then he works
on the relationships and then the pacing of each scene. It's
like dressing the film.

Although Scorsese's film features a single casino, the Tangiers, as
the centrepiece of the story, it represents four that were at the centre of mob activities more than twenty years earlier – the Stardust,
the Frement, the Frontier and the Marina. The director was at
pains to clarify that the scams being run by the mob as featured in
the film had nothing to do with Vegas as it was in 1994. 'That was
twenty years ago, before the old mob lost their control. At that time
every casino was owned by some mob from a different part of the
country.' The Riviera doubled as the fictional Tangiers because it
had been built in the 1970s, and had retained the style which suited
the film perfectly.

Filming in Las Vegas was 'hellish', said Scorsese. 'We had some
problems because the movie is based on real people and a lot of
them are still there. They'd want to hang around to watch us, and
it got really difficult because they were parts of rival factions which
meant they couldn't be on the set at the same time.'

Filming took place during normal working hours, so the casino's
normal activities went on in the background while extras, dressed
in 1970s fashions, filled the foreground. One of the dealers, whom
Scorsese used in the film, had been working there since the 1970s.
He was featured in the scene in which Joe Pesci as Nicky Santoro
and Frank Vincent as Frank Marino come in to play blackjack
despite the fact that Nicky has been banned; they were shooting at
four in the morning and the place was still alive – in the background a real winner was yelling. Pesci set about verbally abusing
the dealer, ad-libbing and throwing the cards at him. It turned out
that the dealer had been in the self-same situation with the real
Tony Spilotro; half-way through the scene, he leaned over to
Scorsese and said, 'You know, the real guy was much tougher with
me. He was really uncontrollable.'

Before filming, Scorsese had met the real-life 'Ace' – Frank 'Lefty' Rosenthal, who was running his own restaurant in a wealthy retirement resort in Florida – and from him he was able to plan how to shoot many of the scenes, particularly the opening sequence in which the car is blown up with 'Ace' Rothstein inside. When the car went up, Rosenthal had first thought it was just an accident; he told Scorsese that the first he knew anything, he saw flames coming out of the air-conditioning unit. 'Then he looked down and saw his arm on fire and he thought of his kids,' said Scorsese. The door had not been closed properly and 'Lefty' was able to roll out and found himself being pulled away by two Secret Service agents who were there checking security in preparation for a visit by Ronald Reagan the following week. 'They pulled him aside and it was only when the car went up that he realized it was intentional.'

With these details, Scorsese decided to show the explosion three times, all in different ways; the third version was the way 'Lefty' remembered it, with all the smaller details.

For Sharon, playing the role of Ginger was quickly turning into the best acting experience she'd ever had. 'She was really great to play because she wasn't a cliché,' she said. 'It wasn't a stereotype based on someone's fantasy of a gangster's moll. And because we had a span of ten years to cover, it was even more interesting.'

Scorsese wanted audiences to really feel for 'Ace' and Ginger, and tried to show how they would have had a better chance of making their marriage work if they had been anywhere else but in Vegas; the city and the way it affected the people there was very important to the story. Said Scorsese, 'I think they may have had a chance if it wasn't for that city and what they were doing in it. Although I think there's something in "Ace's" character that ultimately destroys everything.'

Stone and De Niro tried to bring that aspect of Scorsese's concept into their scenes. Said Sharon, 'I think "Ace" and Ginger really loved each other but had this intense inability to connect, and the more they missed, the more upsetting and desperate it became. I think that they not only loved each other but that they had both reached a point in their lives where they saw an opportunity to be with someone, to have someone. When "Ace" first proposes to

Ginger, he tells her that for him, reaching forty, if you find someone then you try to make it work. And she felt the same.'

'Ace' knows what kind of woman she is, and she makes it clear
exactly *what* she is. Said Scorsese, ' "Ace" says, "I know all the
stories about her, but I don't care. I'm 'Ace' Rothstein and I can
change her." But he couldn't change her. And he couldn't control
the muscle – Nicky – because if you try to control someone like
that, you'll be dead.'

To prepare for her role, Sharon researched the life of the real
Ginger – Geri. She was raised in Sherman Oaks, California, and
went to the same high school as the then unknown Robert Redford.
Her father was a gas-pump attendant, and her mother made extra
cash by taking in ironing. Geri's sister, Barbara, later said, 'We were
probably the poorest family in the neighbourhood. We baby-sat,
raked leaves, fed chickens and rabbits for people – anything to
make a buck.'

Geri became a teenage mother, which didn't make life any easier
on the family, but – determined to find a more lucrative way of life
– she took daughter Robin with her to Las Vegas in 1960. She got
work as a topless dancer and made sure she got to know the high
rollers at the gambling tables. Before long she was earning
megabucks as a hooker. Recalled Frank 'Lefty' Rosenthal, 'She was
a "working girl". She had a couple of guys she went with regularly
and was making around $300,000 a year. She was a girl in love with
money. To her a night was a waste if she didn't go home with cash
in her pocket.'

'Lefty' said he first saw her when he walked into the Tropicana
Club in 1968. He recalled, 'She was a real looker. Statuesque with
great posture.' He was 39, she was 33. 'I had to give her a heart-
shaped diamond pin just to get her to start dating me. When we
were out, she'd ask me for money to give to the powder-room lady
as a tip. I'd give her a $100 bill expecting some change, but she
never brought a cent back.'

They were married on 1st May 1969, in a small chapel inside
Caesar's Palace. They had two children, Steven and Stephanie, but,
according to 'Lefty', Geri continued to 'behave like a hooker',
going to sex parties, drinking heavily and taking drugs. 'Lefty', of

course, was no saint, and he had his own string of affairs. But he was consumed with jealousy and began keeping tabs on her. He even made up her daily schedule and taped it to the fridge; if she was planning on doing anything different, he wanted to know what it was.

When she came home half an hour late after collecting the children from school, he virtually interrogated her. She told him she had been caught at a railway crossing while a very long freight train passed. He checked with the freight yard to confirm the time the train had passed through before he believed her.

Despite all this, they were somehow resigned to staying with each other. But then Geri fell for Tony Spilotro, who was known as Tony 'the Ant' because he was so short at 5 feet 4 inches. He was a sadistic killer whose favourite method was to place a friendly hand on his victim's shoulder before shooting them in the head at point-blank range. He beat one woman until she was unconscious and then put her in a lift, allowing the doors to continuously slam against her head until her skull smashed.

According to Ken Clifford, who was with the Las Vegas police intelligence, 'Spilotro openly flaunted his relationship with Geri. He was saying, "I can do it with Geri and nobody can do anything about it." '

'Lefty' recalled how things came to a head when he saw her drive home drunk from a sexual encounter with 'the Ant'. 'She was pie-eyed, wild. She didn't wait for the garage door to open. She *rammed* it! The neighbours were soon in the street and a couple of cop cars showed up. Geri was about ten feet away from me with a pistol in her hand, aimed at my head. She said she wanted her money or jewellery, or she'd kill me.'

The police arrested her, but on her release she went to the bank to empty safety deposit boxes of $200,000 in cash and $1 million in rubies, sapphires and diamonds.

As the Mafia bosses grew steadily unhappier with the way 'Lefty' was attracting interest from the FBI, and the way 'the Ant' was running wild, they made plans to get rid of them. Consequently, they tried to kill 'Lefty' with a car bomb, and had 'the Ant' beaten with bats and buried in a hole in the desert.

Geri managed to escape to Los Angeles, divorced 'Lefty', spent her money on drugs and alcohol, and ran around with biker gangs for her sexual kicks. She died at the age of 46 from an overdose.

As a character role, Ginger provided Sharon with a challenge that could have been overwhelming had it not been for the ongoing support of Robert De Niro. 'He really helped her through those scenes,' said Scorsese. 'He's very generous with her, and you can see how he's always helping her.'

Sharon also credited De Niro with unyielding support. 'To have a partner like Bob is, you know, a whole different ball game. You can allow yourself the opportunity of stretching yourself, of exposing yourself and going all the way to a different kind of place with your work, and know that you have a wonderful partner like him there.'

To help her further in her performance, she creatively used the clothes that were designed by Rita Ryack and John Dunne. The gold lamé David Bowie-type outfit she wore during the last third of the picture was let out to hang baggy on her, to make her look increasingly thinner from the pills and booze that were wasting her away. As the final act of the picture unfolded, Sharon was called upon to play in a state of self-destruction. 'She did that with her whole body and with the clothes,' said Scorsese, who was delighted with her entire performance. 'It's a very scary role,' he said, 'a tough one, like when she takes cocaine in front of the child. She knew she didn't have to do that scene if she didn't want to, but she chose to do it.'

Sharon insisted that the film wasn't as tough to make as it might have seemed, and said, 'It was actually great fun to shoot. When I did that scene smashing up the car, it was just such a release. I'm sure everyone must have times when they've just wanted to do that, like, "You're really bugging me, take that!" '

Because Scorsese structures his films through every detail, he wanted the clothes to become part of the storyline as it progressed. De Niro had no fewer than fifty-two costume changes, each one designed to reflect what was happening to the character at the time. Owing to last-minute script changes, Ryack and Dunne kept three individual closets of clothes for each of the principal actors. The

basic rule for dressing 'Ace' was that, at the beginning of the story
he wears the traditional dark suit, but as his success grows in Las
Vegas so his clothes become more colourful and ultimately
outrageous. 'We chose the colours very carefully,' said Scorsese.
'Our rituals in the morning, once we narrowed down the idea of
which outfit, were to choose which shirt, then which tie, then
which jewellery.' The outrageous mustard-yellow suit or the navy-
blue silk shirt and navy-blue tie with the crimson jacket, were all
designed to follow 'Ace's' decline as he gradually goes off the rails.
Sharon had fewer costume changes than De Niro – around forty –
and Joe Pesci had only about twenty. But that was all due to the
research the costume designers did. Rita Ryack, like Scorsese, went
to see Frank 'Lefty' Rosenthal, who told her that he never wore the
same outfit twice. Another basic rule, as far as 'Ace's' clothes were
concerned, was that silks, cashmeres and mohairs were the only
fabrics he wore.

Perhaps more than most other directors, Scorsese worked closely
with his costume designers. 'Marty is quite unique among directors,' said Ryack. 'He knows everything there is to know about
men's clothing. He's the best-dressed man in Hollywood.'

For Ryack and Dunne, dressing Sharon was a delight. As a former model, she knew how to *wear* the clothes they tried her out in,
making their task quicker and easier. She also knew that, for this
role, she could not look her best throughout. Said Ryack, 'Her ability to say, "It's okay for me to look really bad in that scene and not
be gorgeous at all times" was an incredible help. There are scenes
where she has to look *really* bad.'

The designers had the added task of creating authentic 1970s
designs – an era not renowned for classic fashions – that would still
look stunning. 'The colours are loud and not tasteful,' Ryack
explained, 'but workmanship and the quality of the fabric make
them beautiful.' The workmanship belonged to the original 1970s
'Sultan of Sequins', Bob Makie, who handmade the costumes worn
by the three principals. The clothes were so good that De Niro and
Stone gratefully accepted their stock of costumes as presents from
the producer, Barbara de Fina. The overall cost of the costumes
came to $1 million.

Production designer Dante Ferratti and Scorsese found suitable houses from the 1950s and 1960s, and dressed them up to reflect 'an era of glitz', as Scorsese put it. Where Ferratti was really creative was in various set designs, such as the bedroom for the scene in which Ginger takes too many pills and gets into an emotional state while 'Ace' tries to comfort her. 'There's something about the way the bed is elevated,' said Scorsese, 'it looks like an imperial bed, a king's or a queen's bed. There's something about the wallpaper, the dishes on the wall, that says a great deal about character. Dante made it regal, not just bad taste – even though some of it is bad taste. That moire silk headboard is a backdrop for a battleground – a silk battleground.'

'What interested me was the idea of excess, no limits. People become successful like in no other city,' said Scorsese, who saw the story as a modern parallel to the rise and fall of Sodom and Gomorrah in the Bible. 'Gaining Paradise and losing it through pride and through greed – it's the old-fashioned Old Testament story. "Ace" is given Paradise on Earth. In fact, he's there to keep everybody happy and keep everything in order. But the problem is that he has to give way at times to certain people and certain pressures, which he won't do because of who he is.'

In keeping with Scorsese's policy on finding the more sympathetic aspects of even the most vile characters, Joe Pesci took every opportunity to add a more humane dimension even in the midst of violent acts, as in the scene in which Nicky kills his victim by putting his head in a vice. Said Scorsese, 'Joe found the human way of playing the scene: "Please don't make me do this." But he's a soldier and he has to take these orders, and he has to get that name, otherwise *his* head is in the vice.'

Scorsese shows Nicky as a father who comes home every morning to make breakfast for his son. 'The real man did that,' the director said.

The film's sex scenes, particularly those between Sharon and Joe Pesci, were shot not to titillate but to illustrate the dangerous background to the affair between Ginger and Nicky. Said Sharon, 'He'll kill her if she doesn't do it. That's why the sex scenes are so charged. I certainly wouldn't call them *love* scenes.' Pesci around twelve inches shorter than Sharon, said, 'Such scenes are not always the easiest to film, but these were unique.'

As Scorsese shot each scene, the footage was rushed to his film editor, Thelma Schoonmaker. In an unusual method of editing, she never read the script but cut the footage together, much as she used to edit documentary films she and Scorsese had worked on many years earlier. Because Scorsese shot in sequence as much as possible, it was a method that was workable, and created a documentary feel to it which he was looking for. He said of this method, 'There's story, but no plot. So what you're following is the beginnings of "Ace" coming to Vegas, then the beginnings of Nicky in Vegas. Then "Ace" is succeeding in Vegas, but what's Nicky doing? He's sandbagging guys.'

It was only when into this process that Scorsese decided to use the scene of the car blowing up to begin the film. Then, with the footage finally assembled into a rough assembly, he was able to see how best to use one of his favourite devices – the voice-over. 'There's something interesting about voice-over,' he said. 'It lets you in on the secret thoughts of the characters, or secret observations by am omniscient viewer. And for me it has the wonderful comforting tone of someone telling you a story.'

He had, in fact, become fascinated with the idea of voice-over – or narration – since seeing Nicholas Ray's biblical epic *King of Kings*, made in 1961. That film had been taken over by MGM half-way through production when producer Samuel Bronston needed extra money to complete the huge project, and the studio subsequently had the script rewritten, then later chopped it up into such a shambles that Nicholas Ray hired Ray Bradbury to write a narration, spoken by Orson Welles, to keep the audience up to date with unresolved plot elements. In particular, the narration gave the audience its insight into Judas Iscariot's motivation for betraying Christ, lending the film a semi-documentary flavour. It was a style device that Scorsese used to great effect in *GoodFellas* and again in *Casino*.

After filming was completed and the cast went home, Scorsese was able to view his assembled footage and begin planning another element that has become quintessential Scorsese – the use of music.

Rather than have an original score composed, he used music of the period, carefully choosing selected pieces to reflect the on-screen action even though it was very often provided purely as source music. Originally Scorsese wanted to use 'The House of the Rising Sun' by The Animals at the beginning of the film, but decided it was better off at the end. 'It has an almost religious quality. It's a warning: "Oh mother, tell your children not to do what I have done." '

Some music remained purely as source music despite what was going on on-screen. Following the scene in which 'Ace' and Nicky argue in the desert, they drive to a garage to talk further. Fleetwood Mac's 'Go Your Own Way' plays on the radio. 'It was a key song of the mid-late seventies,' said Scorsese. 'No matter what the mood of the conversation, that music is playing. We were able to use music at that point to take you further back into the time.'

Scorsese chose from over forty years of music, most of which he was able to obtain permission to use, until he finally had a soundtrack that featured some of the great names of music, including Dean Martin, Otis Redding, Dinah Washington and The Animals. In addition, he decided to begin the film with a classical piece, the 'St Matthew Passion' by Bach, which he chose because, 'For me it's the sense of something grand that's been lost. There was the sense of an empire that had been lost, and it needed music worthy of that.' It was not completely without irony that the real 'Lefty' began his in-house TV station by broadcasting, purely by a technical fault, the film *The Fall of the Roman Empire*, an epic of fallen glory much admired by Scorsese.

He used Bach's music again at the end of the film, followed by Hoagy Carmichael. 'For the splendour of the destruction of this sin city, it has got to be Bach, because the old city is being replaced by something that looks seductive, kiddie-friendly.' Scorsese observed that the Vegas that was standing by the time the film had finished at the end of winter in 1995 was there to seduce 'the very core of America'. He said Vegas was saying, 'While the kids watch the Pirate ride, we'll lose your money.'

This was a facet of the city that Sharon was very aware of when she arrived there for filming. It was some years since she had been there, and she noticed how much it had changed. 'It seemed before

that it had more glamour than it now has. It's become more acces-
sible because it has a kind of MTV glamour. For me, I felt the old
style had a little bit more charm.'

As Ian Christie, writing in *Sight and Sound*, observed, the film
'shows a glittering festering latterday Babylon surrounded by desert,
in which appearance is everything, and nothing is what it seems'.

All those who had decided that Sharon's five minutes of fame were
over before cameras even began rolling on *Casino*, were to get a
shock towards the end of 1994 when *The Specialist* was released.
The public liked it, and went *en masse* to see it.

Of course, the critics slated it. Emma Norman (daughter of BBC
TV's top film critic Barry) wrote in *Screen Mirror*:

> It is an ill-conceived thriller which relies on Sharon Stone's
> legs and Sylvester Stallone's muscle power to pull in the pun-
> ters rather than on any attributes the scriptwriters or director
> have to offer.... The plot is nearly as ludicrous as the script.
> Keeping up with who is crossing and double-crossing whom
> and why X wants Y killed requires concentration – not easy,
> as attention wanders off early on. But Woods is always watch-
> able and, given free reign as he is here, he is magnificently
> evil. It is a film reminiscent of an old-fashioned roller-coaster
> with fast, exciting bits all too often interspersed with bore-
> dom.

Anwar Brett, for *Film Review*, thought the film a 'thoroughly enjoyable "erotic" thriller', and noted 'James Woods' wonderfully sleazy
supporting performance'.

Angie Errico wrote in *Empire*, 'This is, without question, the
most expensive utter twaddle since *Basic Instinct*, and like that
movie is embarrassingly entertaining.... The result is preposter-
ous beyond belief but, somehow, incredibly good fun. The only
unhappy aspect for an otherwise titillated viewer is the tragic spectacle of Steiger, a once great actor, hamming away in a silly role and
sillier accent.'

Embarrassingly or otherwise, audiences were entertained and the film went on to take almost $200 million. Certainly the triumph was more the combination of Stallone and Stone than any individual success, and it proved that – as with most female and indeed many male stars – it often came down to screen *teaming*. Put the right people together in the right vehicle, and people will go to see it, as with Jane Fonda and Donald Sutherland in *Klute*. Put them together again in the wrong picture, as with Fonda and Sutherland in *Steelyard Blue*, and wild horses will not drag people to see it.

Sharon was learning the lesson again with De Niro who, although a great star, did not have success with every one of his films. What she should have learned once and for all was that she too could be a great success if she chose wisely. Not every single film had to be a roaring success, just so long as the commercial flops were interspersed amongst the hits – and if the hits were *really* big, then there would be forgiveness for those that were not.

But, as she had said, by then she had stopped making choices for the public; she was more concerned with proving that she was a capable actress. The dream of being a movie star had long gone. She had every right to take this course. But if her choices, made for herself or otherwise, proved too frequent and too costly, forgiveness would be hard to come by.

Critical and commercial success for *Casino* would certainly make the difference, but she couldn't put her career on hold while waiting. She had to make some good choices now.

12

Awards, Accolades and Derision

Sharon had determined to leave her old image behind for good. 'It's as if she lives in another house,' she said. 'She pretty much has her own life now. It doesn't include me any more. She'd become public domain. We never know what's going to happen. It would be pointless to concern myself with it. Audiences want a resurgence of the old-fashioned movie star. I think they want me to be larger than life.'

She certainly looked her usual glamorous self when she turned up at the Oscars in March 1995, wearing a Vera Wang dress and holding hands with Bob Wagner. She believed that she could remain glamorous in the public eye without resorting to raunchy sex scenes, and she hoped to take even more control over her work. The experience of making *Casino* had boosted her confidence, had stretched her acting muscles, and convinced her that the beautiful blonde from *Basic Instinct* and *Sliver* should remain securely locked away in that other house. In early 1995 she knew it was time to move on from where Martin Scorsese had left her, even though she was yet to hear the critical and public reaction to her performance as Ginger. Despite the warning Joe Eszterhas had given, she was determined there would be no stepping back and playing it safe. 'I think risks are terribly exciting. I'd rather lose than be timid. After all, we're just an amalgamation of our experiences. If you don't take risks, eventually you're nothing.'

She certainly changed her image to appear in the American TV sitcom *Roseanne* as a hard-bitten drunk. Hardly recognizable, she proved her comedy worth by keeping the audience in howls of laughter. Roseanne herself was so impressed that she offered Sharon the role of Patsy in her planned American version of the hit British comedy series *Absolutely Fabulous*. Not wanting to be tied down by TV, however, Sharon wisely and politely turned down the offer.

Looking to the future of her Chaos Productions, she negotiated with Miramax Films a deal to back her own productions; the deal was said to be worth $50 million to Sharon. Harvey Weinstein, co-chairman of Miramax, said, 'There's no star around who's smarter or more glamorous. As the producer, with payments and shares of the profits, she'll be making rather more than peanuts.'

The first film under the new agreement was scheduled to be *Last Dance*, in which she would play a murderess on Death Row – and get paid $6 million. Apart from her own projects, she was still in demand by other companies and, taking a leaf out of Richard Gere's book, she began considering a remake of *Les Diaboliques*. It was a horror classic, made in 1955, about a tyrannical schoolmaster who is murdered by his wife and his mistress. In the ensuing days and weeks, there is increasing evidence that they have botched the job, building to a final chilling fifteen minutes that remains a pure cinema classic when they discover the body of their victim in the bath.

John Badham had already remade the film as *Reflections of Murder*, with Tuesday Weld and Joan Hackett, in 1974. But that was a TV movie, albeit a superior one. Then came another TV version, *House of Secrets*. It seemed to Sharon that there was an opportunity to do it again for mainstream cinema as *Diabolique*. This certainly offered her a meaty role as the murderous mistress, as originally played by Simone Signoret. But there were disagreements over money. Sharon, biding her time and enjoying the opportunity to banter, asked for $5 million; the producers were offering $4 million. Somehow, the final figure arrived at $6 million!

At the same time, Sharon was taking another remake offer very seriously. In 1958 Kim Novak and James Stewart had made an unlikely romantic duo in the comedy *Bell, Book and Candle*. Novak, a blonde star at Columbia, played a modern-day witch who charms Stewart, as a publisher about to marry someone else. Sharon still hoped to remake *Niagara*, and seemed determined to put every effort into redoing *Bell, Book and Candle*. Her fascination with the subject seemed more to do with her need to make iconographic reference points in her life and career rather than anything else, since the original film had been only a modest success. But having refused to portray Marilyn Monroe, and having the chance to be Marlene Dietrich pulled from under her feet, this remake offered an opportunity to walk in footsteps trodden by another star who suffered, like Sharon, from being told she couldn't act. In Novak's case, because she was working under the star system, she was never really given the chance as her studio didn't want to take any risks with her. However, the interesting thing about *Bell, Book and Candle* is that it preceded the re-teaming of Novak and Stewart in Hitchcock's *Vertigo*, which arguably remains Novak's best performance and best film. There may have even been a subconscious reference in Sharon's mind that *Vertigo* had been adapted from the French book *D'entre les Morts* – written by duo authors Pierre Boileau and Thomas Narcejac, who wrote the novel from which *Les Diaboliques* was adapted.

Despite her dedication to finding more interesting and challenging roles to play, her image as the human 'Barbie doll' was still sticking. In an interview in June 1995, in which Simon Rose of *Screen Mirror* asked Theresa Russell if there was more to her than someone who took off her clothes in many of her films, Russell replied, 'Most people would say so, yes. In Hollywood, I've earned a lot of respect. I'm not a big bankable name but I'm also not regarded as the one who can't act but gets her boobs out. I could have taken the Sharon Stone route, but I didn't. I've done much more difficult characters.'

That summer Sharon took *The Quick and the Dead* to Cannes where it was felt – based on past experience – she could get the fullest international attention. On the opening day of the Festival she turned up at a screening of *Catwalk*, perhaps out of sheer nostalgia for the days when she was a model. She arrived wearing Valentino, and managed to overshadow the current crop of supermodels, including Cindy Crawford and Carla Bruni, also dressed in Valentino.

It was at Cannes that Sharon announced that she would be making *Diabolique* and *Bell, Book and Candle*, though she failed to endear herself to the Festival's organizers when she rejected their invitation to feature at an official Palais press conference. But she did come across Paul Verhoeven, there to introduce his 'new Sharon Stone' – Elizabeth Berkley, the unfortunate young star of his biggest disaster ever, *Showgirls*.

On the final day, Sharon was present at the screening of *The Quick and the Dead* which closed the Festival. She had gone there to promote it and felt she could do little more to help the film along. In fact, it had been held back from release by Columbia, anxious that it would get swamped by the flash flood of Westerns in 1994. It was not a success by any standards, taking just $34 million. To many of her detractors, this was proof that she was washed up; but it was hardly conclusive proof that audiences would not accept Sharon in something other than a sexy role. The failure of *The Quick and the Dead* may have had more to do with the fact that it came at the tail-end of a string of Westerns, each of which in turn had proved disastrous. Even the best and most expensive of them all, Kevin Costner's *Wyatt Earp*, flopped. The comeback of the Western had been over-hyped. Every one of them was heralded to rival *Unforgiven*, and in the end none of them did.

The Quick and the Dead was derided by the critics. They refused to take Sharon seriously as a female version of 'The Man With No Name', and the stylized direction of Sam Raimi was criticized for looking like a pastiche of Sergio Leone. 'Despite the authentic cowboy gear,' wrote Simon Rose in *Screen Mirror*, 'and the lean, mean way she draws on a cigarette, Sharon Stone still comes across as Sharon Stone. . . . Although Stone does her best to show she's tough, she remains too much of a movie star to shoot anybody unless it's a fair fight.' He said that although she rides into Redemption to take part in a shooting contest, 'her real aim is to kill Hackman. We know this because she suffers from an acute attack of the dreaded flashbacks whenever he is near.' The use of flashbacks was certainly inspired by Sergio Leone's use of them in his films, and Simon Rose echoed many other critics when he wrote:

> Sam Raimi has unintentionally produced a comedy, a pastiche of the Sergio Leone Spaghetti Western. Unfortunately, while it might have made for an amusing ten minutes, it makes for an incredibly turgid feature-length movie. . . . His ludicrous efforts to make each gunfight seem fresh and exciting rapidly pall and the film is about as taut as an uninflated balloon. *The Quick and the Dead* is not very quick and could hardly be deader. At one point, Stone says, 'I'm through.' More movies like this and she will be.

Perhaps Sharon took comfort from the fact that when *A Fistful of Dollars* was released in America and Britain in 1967, all the critics – virtually without exception – said that Clint Eastwood couldn't act, that Sergio Leone couldn't direct, and that the film would come to nothing. Not that *The Quick and the Dead* is ever likely to achieve the classic status of *A Fistful of Dollars*; it just was not as bad as most critics said. A more balanced review was given in *Film Review* by Marianne Gray who thought it was

> . . . regular straight-ahead Western fare except this gunslinger isn't a gal with a barroom frock and big hair. She's a female Eastwood who can pack one helluva punch. It's a daft film but huge fun. It looks good as painted by comedy-horror master Sam *Evil Dead* Raimi in provocative tones and leery distortions of the prototypes. Stone is OK (looks better than she acts), but Hackman, as the elegant, evil Herod of this particular hellhole, is just great. . . . Definitely a far call from John Ford, this is an uneven, uneasy fantasy that not everybody will enjoy for it is very violent and fairly predictable, but it's a one-off and I enjoyed its oddness. . . . It hits some sort of a mark, even if the mark is a little off the patch.

Despite its failure, the film brought attention to Sharon's brother, Michael, whose criminal background and shady past made for popular copy in the tabloids. In June he announced he was hoping to marry Tamara Beckwith, daughter of British millionaire Peter Beckwith. Despite a broken marriage in his distant past, Michael, like the rest of his siblings, was continually inspired by his parents' successful marriage, and he said, 'It's because of them that I want to marry Tamara. They are still in love, they still hold hands and kiss. Dad gazes at her with this wonderful look in his eye and I've always wanted that.'

Life for Michael had changed for the better, and he always thanked Sharon for her part in that. But he also experienced some of the pressures Hollywood had to offer – particularly that of being Sharon Stone's brother. He was trying to make a career for himself as an actor, and was also having a go at writing scripts. He said, 'When I walk in I feel like I've got a lot more to prove. It's like everyone's waiting for me to fall flat on my face. They all want to know whether I'm going to crash and burn. Well, I tell you what – I'm here for the duration.'

Michael commented, 'Some people are desperate to get to her, and try to do it through me. They'll casually say, "I have this script and there will be a role in it for you if you show it to Sharon." It happened a few months ago, and I told the guy, "I don't need to give my sister a script to get a part in a film. Sharon can't afford to do a lousy film just to give her brother a hand." '

Unfortunately for Michael, Tamara's father did not approve of him, mainly because of his two-year jail term. As any millionaire father would be, Beckwith was also convinced that Michael's interest in his daughter had more to do with her inheritance than real love, and he forbade Tamara to marry him. Consequently, a rift grew between father and daughter, a situation that distressed Michael who had remained close to his own parents despite his wild past.

While Michael was courting Tamara, Sharon was finding herself no nearer to personal satisfaction. She and Bob Wagner had been together for eighteen months, but by July 1995 she seemed to have finally tired of his lack of ambition. It was said that she got 'tired of being in charge. She doesn't want a guy she has to take care of all the time.'

She reportedly told him to leave her house, and gave him an ultimatum to make an effort for himself, give her a baby and marry her. He did move out, and she was said to be upset by the situation, but it seems that he concluded he was willing to comply with her wishes, and so he moved back in.

Kelly had also failed to find marital bliss, despite having become engaged to be married that summer. But six days before the wedding, the ceremony was called off due to 'irreconcilable differences'.

Sharon had been looking for a role that did not require her to look the least bit glamorous, and *Last Dance* – the first film to be made under the agreement between Chaos Productions and Miramax Films – seemed to provide that opportunity. Her character, Cindy Liggett, was a drug-taking outcast who has been in prison on Death Row for twelve years, guilty of murder. There have been a number of stays of execution for her while she transforms herself into a model prisoner, although she is given to complaining that the showing of endless TV quiz shows is more inhuman than Death Row. Then the Governor decides to use her case as an issue in his election campaign by sending her to her execution. A young lawyer, Rick Hayes – played by Rob Morrow from TV's *Northern Exposure* – believes she does not deserve to die and sets about trying to have her sentence commuted.

Not only did Sharon want to come up with a performance to follow Ginger in *Casino* that would give her credibility as an actress she also wanted once and for all to lay the sex symbol image to rest. She said, 'This role offered more truth and simplicity than I've ever been afforded with a character. I like to get the chance as an actress to get under the skin of other kinds of personalities, to find out the way another person thinks without being bound by my own life experience and background. I've never killed anyone, but I had to know how Cindy felt about it.'

In her drive to get 'under Cindy Liggett's skin', she took a leaf from Robert De Niro's book. In the past he had gone to unbelievable lengths to add authenticity to the roles he had played. For

scenes of *Raging Bull* in which, as Jack La Motta, he had to appear
heavy, he put on pounds by gorging himself on the kind of
spaghetti that La Motta actually ate. Sharon didn't need to go to
such extremes, but she did visit a women's jail to talk with a number of convicted killers. She also asked if she could be locked away
for a time in a Death Row cell, and her wish was granted. 'It was
just unbelievable,' she said.

Filming got under way in South Carolina, with Bruce Beresford
directing. Sharon had no qualms about leaving off the lipstick and
foundation to play what was the most unglamorous role of her
career to date. She even dyed her hair a dull, mousy rust colour
and gave it an unkempt, matted look. There were some sugges-
tions that she should pretty herself up a bit, but she was adamant
that she maintain her dour, well-worn look. There remains, however, a train of thought – both in the film business and among
critics – that once a sex symbol, always a sex symbol, and Marilyn
Monroe is cited as someone who tried to turn herself into a serious
actress and failed. More recently there was the case of Julia
Roberts, who flopped as Victorian maid *Mary Reilly*, and Michelle
Pfeiffer was accused of trying to disguise her beauty in dull,
frumpy frocks in *Frankie and Johnny*. But Sharon was inspired by
previous glamour queens who had allowed themselves to go to pot
on screen and triumphed, such as Elizabeth Taylor in *Who's Afraid
of Virginia Woolf?* and Jessica Lange in *Frances*. She might also
have cited Susan Sarandon who was playing a plain-clothed nun in
Dead Man Walking, covering basically the same premise as *Last
Dance* but with a male convict on Death Row helped by a sister of
mercy played by Sarandon.

Ironically – considering the impact that *Dead Man Walking* ultimately had on *Last Dance*, and particularly the competition
Sarandon's performance became for Sharon – Sarandon and her
husband, actor-director Tim Robbins, had been trying to get their
production made for three years. Every studio in town had rejected
it before Britain's own Working Title Films decided to back it.
Susan was more than ten years older than Sharon, and had seen
what it was like to be Hollywood's hottest actress when she starred
with Geena Davis in *Thelma and Louise*, despite having been

around since the 1970s. Neither Sharon nor Susan considered themselves in competition to begin with, but what would later occur could not be described as anything else.

Meanwhile, the 'new Sharon Stone', Elizabeth Berkley, was the current 'pretty young thing' who had scored a success with teenagers on American TV in the comedy series *Saved By the Bell*. In effect, she had taken the Sharon Stone route to which Theresa Russell had referred, by stripping for Paul Verhoeven and Joe Eszterhas in *Showgirls* – which flopped spectacularly, yet somehow failed to damage either Verhoeven's or Eszterhas's viability. Verhoeven was announcing that Elizabeth would reveal all once more in *All About Eve*. Around the same time, another of the 'Showgirls', Gina Gershon, was being slated to star in the new Eszterhas screenplay, *Original Sin*, which Sharon had considered and turned down.

If anyone was warning Sharon to watch her back as much younger pretenders threatened to take her place, she was telling them the girls were welcome to it.

In December 1995 it was reported that Sharon had miscarried only three weeks after discovering she was pregnant. She was, said a friend, 'devastated. She had been absolutely thrilled to find that she was pregnant. She may have given the impression of being tough and ambitious, but she was longing to give birth.'

For the first three weeks, Sharon had been planning how to work around the pregnancy, and had started a new regime of healthy eating and keeping fit. She told friends that she was prepared to give up the prospect of earning millions to become a mother. But she lost her baby. The tragedy was said to have made her all the more determined to have her own child, and she had even begun to talk about adopting. But ultimately, the loss of the baby spelled the end of the romance between Sharon and Bob.

Despite her grief, and in part to help overcome it, she threw herself into her next film, *Diabolique*. When producers Marvin Worth and James G. Robinson, and director Jeremiah Chechik chose to remake the French horror classic, they decided they needed something new to the plot to provide a 1996 audience with a twist the 1955 audience didn't have.

The story was basically the same. Guy Barab, played by Chazz Palmenteri, runs his school (St Anselm's School for Boys) with an iron rod, having paid for it with money from his rich but ailing wife, Mia, played by Isabelle Adjani. He has an abusive affair with one of his teachers, Nicole – Sharon Stone – who persuades Mia that they should murder him. Mia goes to stay with Nicole at her apartment, where Guy turns up to beg her to return to him. Mia gives him a drink which she had drugged, and then the two women drown him in the bathtub. They dump his body in the school swimming-pool; but when the pool is later drained, it is not to be found.

Mia's heart condition is not helped by sporadic and fleeting appearances of Guy, and she is made even more nervous by Shirley Vogel (Kathy Bates), a retired policewoman who works as a private investigator. The classic, climactic moment – that had audiences screaming in 1955 – comes when Guy's body is discovered by Mia in the bathtub where they had drowned him. As he sits up, she suffers a heart attack. It turns out that Nicole and Guy have conspired to murder Mia by giving her a heart attack and so inherit her money.

For the American remake, it was thought that the ending was too bleak; the producers wanted the film to conclude without losing sympathy for Nicole, especially if she was being played by Sharon Stone. And so in a new twist, Mia survives the heart attack, and Nicole finds herself unable to go on with the ploy. Instead, she joins Mia in the real murder of Guy. Then they realize they have been discovered by Shirley, but she finally helps them to cover up their crime.

For Sharon, playing Nicole was a far, far cry from playing Catherine Tramell or Carly Norris, and she relished it. During an interview given on the set, she finished explaining how she and Isabelle Adjani plot to kill Chazz Palmenteri by rubbing her hands with glee. 'Bad girls are more fun to play,' she said, 'because the boundaries are so much broader. They're just so much fun to play.'

When the oft-raised subject of plastic surgery came up, she said, 'I think about having plastic surgery every twenty minutes, wondering which part of me is slipping away and I can fix it. But I've realized I never got interesting parts until I grew into myself.'

Having played in succession three women who were law-breakers, immoral and in the last two cases murderous, did she have a problem coming to terms with the morality of these characters? 'You cannot play a character from a judgmental position. You just have to sort of surrender yourself to it.'

Despite the grim premise of the story, on the set there was a sense of camaraderie and playfulness between the three principals. Said Palmenteri, 'Well, how would you like to have to go to work and make love to Isabelle one day and Sharon the next?' He maintained his sense of humour even after shooting the two scenes in which he is drowned in the bath, saying, 'It was hard, going from dry to wet, from wet to dry, being drowned constantly.'

Of Isabelle Adjani – who had been requested by Michael Douglas to play Catherine in *Basic Instinct* – Sharon said, 'I think the chemistry between us is very good, so it's a real joy to be working with her. As a matter of fact I'd tried to work with her before and had requested she be cast in another film but it didn't work out.' In the original film there was a definite lesbian undercurrent between the two women. In this 1990s version, that aspect was more of an overtone. Sex and nudity was there in the film, more of it coming from Isabelle Adjani than from Sharon.

For anyone who had not seen the original, this re-telling was a good, chilling yarn. But neither the film nor the actors were well served by their director, whose previous career highlights were the comedies *National Lampoon's Christmas Vacation* and *Benny and Joon*. Nevertheless, there were some fine production values and the whole thing, while firmly set in the 1990s, has a look and feel that is almost retro-1950s, as though it were paying homage to the original.

The year ended on a high note for Sharon, as she received her own star on Hollywood Boulevard's legendary Walk of Fame. Cynics were not slow to point out that the movie stars who have had their own pavement stars paid for them – the estimated cost was around $3,000, which is a drop in the ocean when you're a millionaire. In actuality, any actor who wants a pavement star has to be nominated, usually by a studio (sometimes in more contrived instances by the PR company employed by the actor), and then they have to be approved by a Hollywood Chamber of Commerce committee which decides if the nominee is worthy of such an honour. In Sharon's case, they decided she was, and the day before *Casino* opened she was accompanied by Martin Scorsese to unveil the star. She said, 'I'm very happy for this kind of acknowledgment that the public is happy with my work.'

Casino was released to a mixed bag of reviews in America at the end of 1995. Some critics liked it, and some absolutely hated it. Some described it as a careless remake of *GoodFellas*; most thought it was too long at three hours. They did like the acting, though, and Sharon Stone received the first really good personal notices of her career. Audiences were good, but not overwhelming. Scorsese was philosophical about it all. 'What can I do?' he asked. 'The movie's the movie. If it's gonna play it's gonna play. If it's not gonna play it's not gonna play. If people don't like it, what can I do about it?' He didn't have to do too much. Word of mouth and the controversial content of the film helped to swell the takings.

In quick succession, as 1995 turned into 1996, Sharon was nominated for both a Golden Glove and an Oscar for her performance in *Casino*. Susan Sarandon was also nominated for both awards for her *Dead Man Walking*, which had been released before *Last Dance* and was proving extremely successful to the delight of Working Title Films. Both the film and Sarandon's performance were now hot competition for Sharon on two fronts: the success of *Last Dance* and her performance in *Casino*. Sharon was now into a whole new Hollywood ball-game.

When *Casino* was released in Britain in early 1996, it received a far better critical reception than on its home soil. More often than not, Sharon surprised the British critics. Simon Rose, in *Screen Mirror*, raved, 'While we expect De Niro and Pesci to be good, Stone is a revelation as the flash, fragile Ginger. She emerges here as an actress of stature who, amazingly, steals the movie from her co-stars. In my book, she is more than worthy of an Oscar.' But he had reservations about the whole film, which he said, 'Certainly is a skilfully-made movie, with its neon title sequence among the greatest openings ever made. . . . However, three hours is a long time and I never found myself caught up in the rambling story. My major criticism, though, is the film's violence. Three scenes in particular are horrendously and disgustingly explicit. Would the censor have passed them if it had been anyone other than Martin Scorsese? I doubt it.'

Empire's Philip Thomas was another surprised critic. 'Sharon Stone is a revelation,' he said. With less surprise, he added, 'This is De Niro's finest hour certainly since *GoodFellas* and maybe since *The King of Comedy*. On screen for nearly the whole three-hour running time, he is chillingly logical about his life at first, slowly descending into panic, frustration and violence as things go wrong. . . . Pesci is his usual mesmerizing self, and if at times the story drags – with too much voice-over and quasidocumentary – the three of them refuse to let go of your nether regions for a second.'

Empire reviewed it again later for its video release, and Neil Jeffries thought that Stone was 'the film's touchstone, acting even better than she looks'. He wrote:

You can say what you like about this being *GoodFellas Part 2* or *GoodFellas in Vegas*, but it's impossible not to be impressed. . . . Ultimately, the film is a simple story of a gambler's struggle to hold his life together against the odds, but the scope of Scorsese's masterful vision escalates this to a work of art. . . . Whether it's Pesci and Stone, Stone and De Niro or De Niro and Pesci, the electricity generated is more than enough to sustain this through its lengthy running time. Okay, so it might have worked just as well if an hour shorter, but complaining that this numbs your arse is like whinging that the roof of the Sistine Chapel gives you a crick in the neck.

Marianne Gray of *Film Review* noted that 'unflagging as the Ace story is, even more intriguing are the subplots, the character studies and environment moves in this fascinating epic, all brilliantly scripted for fast action and filled out by an extraordinary soundtrack.' As far as performances were concerned, Ms Gray said, 'De Niro and Pesci are on form and it is good to see James Woods in a decent film.' But, like a handful of critics, she seemed to begrudge Sharon a really good notice, saying, 'She does a pretty good job in her first "great" performance as Ginger, the ex-hooker turned class-act destined to demise sunk in pills and liquor, but I have my reservations about the role itself, which, compared to De Niro's and Pesci's, seemed a little predictable. But maybe that's how it was in the original story. I wish her well.'

Scorsese's intention to maintain Ginger as a character who is seen through the eyes of 'Ace' and Nicky was a point that Jonathan Romney did not miss in his review in *Sight and Sound*: 'Ginger, as we might expect in a Scorsese film, is *Casino*'s blind spot; we are told less about her than about "Ace" and Nicky, and she is never the narrator. She is first seen turning "tricks", in both the gaming and prostitution senses; clearly, she is as skilled and as driven an operator as "Ace" himself. But he sees her as the random factor personified.' Romney was one critic far less concerned with the performances of the three principals than with the film's overall effect:

> *Casino* is the flashiest, most superficial film Martin Scorsese has ever made – which is to say, it serves its theme brilliantly. . . . This prodigal film invites a proliferation of readings – in terms of character, of visual style, of narrative construction, of gambling theory, of Scorsesean religious-ethical debate, and of cinema itself. Among other things *Casino* is an allegorical account of the dangerous seductiveness of Hollywood cinema, another strident mechanism for harvesting dollars. It constantly dazzles with visuals, auditory and thematic stimuli.

Other reviews were generally enthusiastic. Jonathan Ross called it 'a genuine classic' in the *News of the World*, hailing it as 'a stunning feat of film-making', and Steve Wright in the *Sun* thought it was 'Scorsese's finest movie yet'.

When the Golden Globes ceremony arrived in January, the odds seemed to be on Susan Sarandon winning Best Actress. Second favourite was British star Emma Thompson for *Sense and Sensibility*; but instead of winning for her performance, Emma won for her writing of the screen adaptation. Against all the odds, Best Actress went to Sharon Stone, who burst into tears and cried, 'It's a miracle. I'm so proud to work with people of the quality and calibre of this group that made *Casino*, a five-month-long project that we all put our hearts and soul and blood and sweat into.' It may have sounded typical Hollywood ballyhoo, but in a sense Sharon had been striving for this moment all her life, and she undoubtedly meant what she said from the heart. Now the odds were on her winning the Oscar, if for no other reason than that the Oscars usually reflected the Golden Globes.

Michael Stone was back in the news in February when he announced that he would marry Tamara Beckwith. It had taken some time, but Tamara had finally convinced her father, Peter, that she really was in love with Michael, and that they would not be separated. Michael also convinced him that he was not interested in Tamara's inheritance by agreeing to sign an agreement waiving any right to her wealth should they divorce. The rift between father and daughter was healed. Michael's only disappointment was that in all the years since his first divorce, he had not been able to see his only son.

The Stone family had maintained their closeness. Younger brother Patrick had managed to remain largely anonymous, but Kelly had a more public profile, mainly because she had wanted to let the world know how much her big sister had helped her through troubled times. 'Like all sisters, Sharon and I have had our spats,' said Kelly, 'but at the end of the day we are friends. We swap clothes – but hers are designer dresses worth thousands.'

The 68th American Academy Awards were held on 25th March, hosted by Whoopie Goldberg. It was one of the most memorable Oscar events in years, with a surprising and moving appearance by Christopher Reeve in a wheelchair, his neck broken in a fall from a horse several months earlier. Also there was Kirk Douglas, his face still partly paralysed by a stroke, to collect a special Oscar. When the time came to announce Best Actress, the nominees all tried to look relaxed: Sharon Stone, Susan Sarandon, Emma Thompson for *Sense and Sensibility*, and Meryl Streep for *The Bridges of Madison County*. It was a formidable group, and there were no clear favourites. The winner, ultimately was Susan Sarandon. The fact that Sharon lost in such company, and the mere fact of being nominated at all, meant that from then on she would no longer be just another sex bombshell but 'Oscar nominee Sharon Stone'. On the other hand, it could be argued that in Hollywood, where all they care about are the winners, a single Oscar win for *Casino* would have added to its already impressive performance at the box office. More than that, it would have meant absolutely everything to Sharon's credibility to have been able to walk away with the much coveted golden man.

Last Dance was released to disastrous reviews, both in America and in Britain. Simon Rose, of *Screen Mirror*, forgot all about his praise for Sharon's performance in *Casino*, and wrote, 'Heaven preserve us from sex bombs who want to Act. Sharon Stone's career was going nowhere in dire movies such as *Police Academy 4*. Then she left her knickers in her handbag while filming that scene in *Basic Instinct* and suddenly she's so hot she's scorching the audience's fingers. Instead of capitalizing on this, she wants to play parts that stretch her. But the only thing that's stretched is our patience. Does anybody really want to see superstar Stone as an unsympathetic prisoner awaiting execution?' He went on to say, in what was a kind of backhanded compliment, 'Although Stone's acting is competent, you never believe she's anything other than Sharon Stone playing a part.'

In a sense, that critic had hit upon the problem, but it had nothing to do with Sharon's inability to act. It was simply that she had made such an impact as a sex symbol that neither the critics nor the public were prepared to give her a chance. She *was* good in the film; the film was *not* paricularly good. It suffers from a dull script and equally dull direction. It was also overshadowed by *Dead Man Walking*. But even without Susan Sarandon's superior film, *Last*

Dance, while not the disaster critics considered it, was just not good enough to do really well. Even so, the truth seemed to be that Sharon Stone was on a hiding to nothing, and most critics, despite their initial surprise at how good she was in *Casino*, were not prepared to allow her to prove herself a second time.

Barry Norman was even more scathing: 'Since her sudden rise to notoriety with *Basic Instinct* in 1992, she's made eight films, and with the exception of *Casino* every one a bummer.' He described *Last Dance* perhaps accurately as a 'fourth division version of *Dead Man Walking*', and summed up his opinion of the film with:

Stone's the prisoner on Death Row and Rob Morrow is an inexperienced but dedicated and indeed snivelling young lawyer trying to save her. Do we care? No, not a lot. The thing about Sharon Stone is that she's only a star when she's exuding sex. Here, with mousy hair and shapeless clothes, she's called upon to exude acting, and that's another matter. I'm not saying she can't act; she can, and *does*. Every gesture, every facial expression is straight out of the acting by numbers book, and you can watch it happening. But the best actors transcend acting and make you believe they are what they're playing. Stone can't do that.

In unusually quick succession, the release of *Diabolique* followed, splitting the critics. 'An edge of your seat film,' is how *More* described it, while *WKDM-AM* in America said it was, 'a stunning, tantalizing, triumphant mystery thriller (with) sexual, powerful performances'.

But the majority of critics compared it with the original, which meant that in most cases the film was bound to lose by sheer comparison. 'This is a remake of the terrifying *Les Diaboliques*,' began Simon Rose in *Screen Mirror*, adding, 'but it's scarier to ponder how so much talent can make something so dull. . . . Forget goosebumps – everything is spelled out. And it's impossible to believe in Stone when she teaches in sleeveless cocktail dresses. Only Kathy Bates as a jokey detective shines.'

'Henri-Georges Clouzot's *Les Diaboliques* is such a widely imitated work that a remake seems superfluous,' wrote Kim Newman for *Sight and Sound*, going on to list numerous films including *Hush Hush, Sweet Charlotte* and *Deathtrap*.

> For most of its length, *Diabolique* is merely a crass and inept reproduction of the original. Chazz Palmenteri, replacing Paul Meurisse, comes off best as the utter bastard who mistreats both his women. The two women are more problematic, though they would seem to be well cast. Adjani certainly has the fragility and heartbreaking timidity of Vera Clouzot, and Sharon Stone's incipiently matronly mistress slyly approaches Simone Signoret's image while remaking herself. However, neither actress is well served by the direction of Jeremiah Chechik which seems to go out of its way to show them in a (literal) bad light. . . . The strength of Clouzot's *Les Diaboliques* is that it is consistently surprising, a factor which cannot be carried over into a carbon copy remake. . . . *Diabolique* opts to look like a horror film. This wouldn't be such a problem if it managed to be scary, but the effect is yet another botched Hollywood shocker.

For good measure, Kim Newman finished her review with, 'This is insulting twaddle.'

By April 1996, Sharon had a new man in her life, ex-basketball player Brad Johnson. It was a short-lived affair. Kelly said that neither she nor Sharon had managed to settle down because they were both searching for old-fashioned men with old-fashioned good manners – someone, in fact, just like their father. Said Kelly, 'We want someone with drive and a strong work ethic who courts us and treats us like ladies. I think the bill is pretty steep and it's hard for us to find a relationship that lives up to our parents' marriage. After 46 years, they are still the loves of each other's lives. They lie together on the sofa to watch TV, kiss each other hello and goodbye and say they love each other ten times day. I don't know if such a relationship exists in the nineties.'

Kelly, no longer confined to her wheelchair, had spent the past three years running Planet Hope and was literally – as her father had always hoped – standing on her own two feet. And nobody could accuse Sharon of relying on others to get ahead, so when she had a relationship, it was for no other purpose than looking for Mr Right. She once joked, 'One thing I find since becoming famous is that I get to torture a higher class of man than I used to.'

There was certainly no shortage of men ready, willing but not necessarily able to date Sharon Stone. 'One thing I've learned is that any man in Hollywood will meet me if I want that. No, make that any man *any*where!'

In May a curious thing happened to Sharon while she was shopping at a chic boutique in Los Angeles. She was in the changing room when a woman approached her and asked her to sign a pair of panties for her husband. This was too much even for someone with Sharon's sense of humour, and she refused the request.

In July, a man whom Sharon thought was a stalker hanging around outside her home could have considered himself lucky not to be blown away by one of her two shotguns. Discovering the 'stalker', she called the police, who arrived and arrested him. It turned out he was a private detective hired by a Hollywood executive who didn't believe her when she said she was unwell and couldn't attend his film gala. This was the sort of incident that made her more determined to move away from Hollywood, but she had yet to commit to such a change.

In September, Sharon had a French lover, 46-year-old Michel Benasera. After just a whirlwind six weeks' romance, they flew to Paris for a weekend; over dinner in an exclusive restaurant, he asked her to marry him, offering her a fabulous diamond engagement ring. Sharon, as impulsive in love as ever, said yes.

They spent the next two weeks on holiday in Marrakech, Morocco, where they rented a £1,000-a-night suite in the Mamounia Hotel. For the first two days they stayed in their room, living on room service; the only person who saw them was the maid who came in to clean the bathroom. The French magazine *Voici* managed to get a few pictures of the couple, but they looked far from happy together. There followed a sudden departure from the

hotel, Benasera flying back to New York and Sharon to Los
Angeles. Apparently, she had given back his ring after a bust-up,
and yet again another romance was over.

Although she had been given a certain amount of power and influ-
ence through her Chaos Productions company, Sharon admitted, 'I
find the business aspects a grind.' Film projects still hung in the
balance; *Niagara* and *Bell, Book and Candle* were still pet ideas, and
she was constantly in demand. In July she finally settled on her
next film; Oliver Stone's *Stray Dogs*, co-starring Nick Nolte.
Working for Stone – director of such films as *Platoon, JFK* and
Nixon – was, for her, as important as it had been to work for Martin
Scorsese. So important, in fact, that she agreed to do it for a relatively tiny fee, around a quarter of a million dollars.

What she would make after *Stray Dogs* remained to be decided.
She still hoped to remake *Niagara*, but in late 1996 she was competing with Linda Fiorentino for Monroe's role. While in Paris in
September, she announced that she would star in an Italian production portraying yet another glamorous screen star, Grace Kelly.
She had great fun teasing the media by wearing what appeared to
be a large wedding ring, prompting rumours that she had secretly
married. But this turned out to be just an elaborate friendship ring.

Despite those who said she was no longer a Hollywood contender, she came out well in a list compiled by Britain's film trade
publication *Screen International*, showing how much each star's
name was expected to do for a film's box office, based on the past
three releases. Sharon came 20th with an average box office of £46.7
million, one place below Sylvester Stallone and above (among
others) Mel Gibson and Michael Douglas, and way above a host of
her female peers including Demi Moore (26th with £42.1 million),
Michelle Pfeiffer (27th with £41.4 million), Sandra Bullock (28th
with £36.8 million), Meryl Streep (30th with £34.9 million), Meg
Ryan (34th with $32.3 million), Sigourney Weaver (45th with £17.5
million), Susan Sarandon (46th with £14.5 million) and Julia
Roberts coming in at 50th with £7.9 million. All the names above
Sharon were male, except for Jodie Foster who was placed 17th

with £53.3 million. Despite the critics, despite the detractors, depite the failure to make one big box-office blockbuster after another, Sharon Stone had become the second biggest female star in Hollywood. Whether she can sustain that or improve on it remains to be seen.

Of course, the thing about Sharon Stone was that she did not get anywhere by being faint-hearted. Nor could she be what many critics claimed she was – a sexy actress with no real talent. She had proved herself capable of an award-winning performace – indeed, the critics had been generally unanimous in their praise for her as Ginger in *Casino* – and she had taken risks in the kind of work she'd chosen to do, even if it had not always paid off. Which meant that as long as she was prepared to continue to take risks, and as long as there were directors of the calibre of Martin Scorsese or Oliver Stone willing to take a risk on her, she would be around for a lot longer than even Joe Eszterhas ever thought.

Bibliography and Sources

Much of the book is the result of formal interviews and sometimes informal talks with numerous people, famous and unknown, who have worked with Sharon Stone, including Michael Douglas, J. Lee Thompson, Richard Chamberlain, Wes Craven, Martin Scorsese, Christian Slater, Sam Wanamaker, Herbert Lom, Steven Seagal and Robert Evans. While I could find no significant references to Sharon Stone in other books, Alan Lawson's biography *Michael Douglas* (Robert Hale, 1993) gave me some additional insights into the background of *Basic Instinct*. More generalised film reference books were useful, particularly, as always Halliwell's *Filmgoer's Companion* (HarperCollins), Virgin's excellent annual *Film Yearbook*, and F. Maurice Speed's yearly *Film Review* (Columbus Books). Also invaluable were the following articles:

Acting On Instinct by Edward Murphy, *Film Review*, May 1992
Bad Girl Makes Good by Edward Peterborough, *Film Review*, March 1996
Don't Call Me a Lady by Leon Wagener, *Sunday Magazine*, 4 October 1992
It's a Blast by Jeff Dawson, Empire, January 1995
Martin Scorsese's Testament by Ian Christie, *Sight & Sound*, January 1996
My Susperstar Sister by Judy McGuire, Sunday Mirror, 4 June 1995

Naked Hollywood by Jenny Cooney, *Empire*, June 1992
Sharon Saved Me by Tanith Carey, *Daily Mirror*, 29 April 1996
Sharon Stone by Stephen Rebello, *Empire*, January 1993
Sharon Stone Age by Allan Hall, *Daily Mirror*, 23 January 1995
Sly Romancing the Stone by Douglas Thompson, *Sunday Mirror Magazine*, 3 July 1994
Someone To Look At by Lizzie Francke, *Sight & Sound*, March 1996
Total Recall, Total Arnie by Anne Thompson, *Empire*, August 1990

Filmography

Stardust Memories 1980. United Artists/Jack Rollins, Charles H. Joffe. Produced by Robert Greenhut. Written and directed by Woody Allen. Starring: Woody Allen, Charlotte Rampling, Jessica Harper, Marie-Christine Barrault, Helen Hanft, Amy Wright, Tony Roberts, Sharon Stone.

Deadly Blessing 1981. Polygram. Directed by Wes Craven. Starring: Maren Jensen, Susan Buckner, Sharon Stone, Lois Nettleton, Jeff East, Ernest Borgnine, Lisa Hartman.

Irreconcilable Differences 1984. Hemdale/Lantana/Warner/Guild. Directed by Charles Shyer. Produced by Alex Winitsky. Screenplay by Nancy Meyers and Charles Shyer. Starring: Ryan O'Neal, Shelley Long, Drew Barrymore, Sam Wanamaker, Allen Garfield, Sharon Stone, Hortensia Colorado, Richard Michenberg, Lorinne Vozoff, Stuart Pankin, David Graf, Jenny Gago.

King Solomon's Mines 1985. Cannon. Directed by J. Lee Thompson. Produced by Menahem Golan and Yoram Globus. Screenplay by Gene Quinitano and James R. Silke, based on the book by H. Rider Haggard. Starring: Richard Chamberlain, Sharon Stone, Herbert Lom, John Rhys-Davies, Ken Gampu, June Buthelezie.
Allan Quartermain and the Lost City of Gold 1987. Cannon.

Directed by Gary Nelson (additional scenes directed by Newt Arnold). Produced by Menahem Golan and Yoram Globus. Screenplay by Gene Quintano, based on the book *Allan Quartermain* by H. Rider Haggard. Starring: Richard Chamberlain, Sharon Stone, James Earl Jones, Henry Silver, Robert Donner, Doghmi Larbi, Aileen Marson, Cassandra Peterson, Martin Rabbett.

Cold Steel 1987. Cinetel. Directed by Dorothy Puzo. Starring: Brad Davis, Sharon Stone, Jonathan Banks, Adam Ant.

Police Academy 4: Citizens on Patrol 1987. Warner Brothers. Directed by Jim Drake. Produced by Paul Maslansky. Screenplay by Neal Israel, Pat Proft and Hugh Wilson. Starring: Steve Guttenberg, Bubba Smith, Michael Winslow, David Grat; Tim Kazurinsky, Sharon Ston, G.W. Bailey, George Gaynes, Bobcat Goldthwait, Leslie Easterbrook.

Action Jackson 1988. Silver Pictures/Lorimar. Directed by Craig R. Baxley. Starring: Carl Weathers Vanity, Sharon Stone, Thomas F. Wilson, Bill Duke, Robert Davi, Jack Thibeau, Craig T. Nelson.

Above the Law (aka *Nico*) 1988. Warner Brothers. Written, produced and directed by Andrew Davis. Starring: Steven Seagal, Pam Grier, Henry Silva, Sharon Stone, Daniel Faraldo, Nicholas Kusenko, Ron Dean.

Beyond the Stars (aka *Personal Choice*) 1989. Sony. Directed by David Saperstein. Starring: Christian Slater, Martin Sheen, F. Murray Abraham, Olivia D'Abo, Sharon Stone, Robert Foxworth.

Total Recall 1990, Carolco. Directed Paul Verhoeven. Produced by Buzz Feitshans and Ronald Shusett. Screenplay by Ronald Shusett, Dan O'Bannion and Gary Goldman, adapted from the short story *I Can Get It For You Wholesale* by Phillip K. Dick. Starring: Arnold Schwarzenegger, Rachel Ticotin, Sharon Stone, Ronny Cox, Michael Ironside, Marshall Bell, Rosemary Dunsmore,

Mel Johnson Jnr, Michael Champion.

Year of the Gun 1991. J & M/Initial/First Indepenent. Directed by John Frankenheimer. Produced by Edward R. Pressman. Screenplay by David Ambrose from the novel by Michael Mewshaw. Starring: Andrew McCarthy, Valerie Golino, Sharon Stone, John Pankow, George Marchell, Mattia Sbragia.

He Said, She Said 1991. Paramount. Directed by Ken Kwapsis and Maisa Silver. Produced by Frank Mancuso Junior. Screenplay by Brian Hohfeld. Starring: Kevin Bacon, Elizabeth Perkins, Nathan Lane, Anthony LaPaglia, Sharon Stone, Stanley Anderson.

Scissors 1991. DDM Film Corp. Directed by Frank De Felita. Starring: Steve Railsback, Sharon Stone, Ronny Cox.

Diary of a Hitman 1991. Continental/Vision Int. Directed by Roy London. Starring: Forrest Whitaker, Sharon Stone, Sherilyn Fenn.

Where Sleeping Dogs Lie 1991. Columbia TriStar. Directed by Charles Finch. Starring: Dallas McDermott, Sharon Stone.

Basic Instinct 1991. Carolco/TriStar. Directed by Paul Verhoeven. Produced by Allan Marshall. Screenplay by Joe Eszterhas. Starring: Michael Douglas, Sharon Stone, Jeanne Tripplehorn, Leilani Sarelle, George Dzunda, Dorothy Malone.

Sliver 1993. Robert Evans/Paramount. Directed by Phillip Noyce. Produced by Robert Evans. Screenplay by Joe Eszterhas, from the novel by Ira Levin. Starring: Sharon Stone, William Baldwin, Tom Berenger, Martin Landau, Nina Foch.

Intersection 1994. Bud Yorkin/Paramount. Directed by Mark Rydell. Produced by Bud Yorkin. Starring: Richard Gere, Sharon Stone, Lolita Davidovich, Martin Landau, David Selby, Meaghan Eastman.

The Quick and the Dead 1994. Columbia/TriStar. Directed by Sam

Raimi. Screenplay by Simon Moore. Starring: Sharon Stone, Gene Hackman, Leonardo DeCaprio, Russel Crowe, Tom Skerrit, Pat Hingle, Woody Strode, Michael Stone.

The Specialist 1994. Warner Brothers. Directed by Luis Llosa. Produced by Jerry Weintraub. Screenplay by Alexandra Seros. Starring: Sylvester Stallone, Sharon Stone, James Woods, Rod Steiger, Eric Roberts.

Casino 1995. Universal/Syalis D.A/Legende Enterprises. Directed by Martin Scorsese. Produced by Barbara de Fina. Screenplay by Nicholas Pileggi and Martin Scorsese, from the book by Nicholas Pileggi. Starring: Robert De Niro, Sharon Stone, Joe Pesci, James Woods, Don Rickles, Alan King, Kevin Pollack, L.Q. Jones, Dick Smothers, Frank Vincent.

Last Dance 1996. Touchstone Pictures. Directed by Bruce Beresford. Produced by Steven Haft. Screenplay by Ron Koslow. Starring: Sharon Stone, Rob Morrow, Randy Quaid, Peter Gallagher, Jack Thompson, Jayne Brook.

Diabolique 1996. Warner/Morgan Creek/Marvin Worth/Goldworth/ABC. Directed by Jeremiah Checkik. Produced by Marvin Worth and James G. Robinson. Screenplay by Don Ross, based on the novel *Celle qui n'etait plus* by Pierre Boileau and Thomas Narcejac, and the screenplay *Les Diaboliques* by Henri-Georges Clouzer. Starring: Sharon Stone, Isabelle Adjani, Chazz Palminteri, Kathy Bates, Spaldin Gray, Shirley Knight, Allen Garfield.

Index